EYEWITNESS

CRYSTAL & GEM

Apatite

Cut topazes

Danburite

Chalcedony

Opal

Calcite

Sphaerocobaltite

Crocoite

EYEWITNESS
CRYSTAL & GEM

Written by
Dr. R.F. SYMES and Dr. R.R. HARDING

Dumortierite bottle

Cut garnets

Cut tourmalines

Aragonite

Microcline

Meta-tobernite

DK

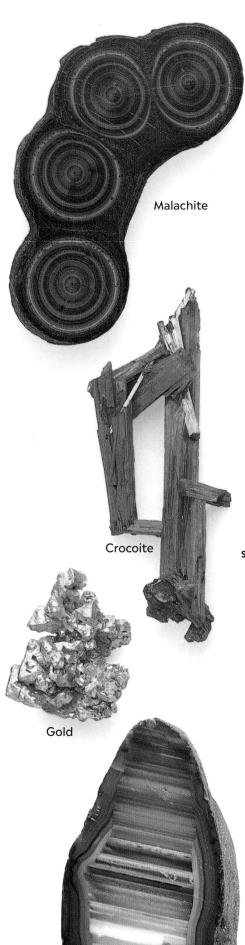

Malachite

Crocoite

Gold

Agate

Cut tourmaline

Cut topaz

Cut sapphire

Mother-of-pearl

Tourmaline

Agate

REVISED EDITION

DK DELHI
Senior Editor Virien Chopra
Senior Art Editor Vikas Chauhan
Art Editor Tanvi Sahu
Assistant Editor Zarak Rais
Assistant Art Editor Prateek Maurya
Picture Researcher Vishal Ghavri
Managing Editor Kingshuk Ghoshal
Managing Art Editor Govind Mittal
DTP Designers Pawan Kumar, Ashok Kumar
Jacket Designer Juhi Sheth
Senior Jackets Coordinator Priyanka Sharma Saddi

DK LONDON
Senior Editor Carron Brown
Art Editor Chrissy Checketts
US Executive Editor Lori Cates Hand
Managing Editor Francesca Baines
Managing Art Editor Philip Letsu
Production Editor Gillian Reid
Production Controller Jack Matts
Senior Jackets Designer Surabhi Wadhwa-Gandhi
Jacket Design Development Manager Sophia MTT
Publisher Andrew Macintyre
Associate Publishing Director Liz Wheeler
Art Director Karen Self
Publishing Director Jonathan Metcalf

Consultant Cally Oldershaw

FIRST EDITION
Project Editor Louise Pritchard
Art Editor Thomas Keenes
Senior Editor Helen Parker
Senior Art Editors Julia Harris, Jacquie Gulliver
Production Louise Barrat
Picture Research Cynthia Hole
Special Photography Colin Keates ABIPP (Natural History Museum)

This Eyewitness ® Guide has been conceived by
Dorling Kindersley Limited and Editions Gallimard

This American Edition, 2023
First American Edition, 1991
Published in the United States by DK Publishing
1745 Broadway, 20th Floor, New York, NY 10019

Copyright © 1991, 2002, 2007, 2014, 2023
Dorling Kindersley Limited
DK, a Division of Penguin Random House LLC
23 24 25 26 27 10 9 8 7 6 5 4 3 2 1
001–335459–Aug/2023

A catalog record for this book is available
from the Library of Congress.
ISBN 978-0-7440-8154-1 (Paperback)
ISBN 978-0-7440-8155-8 (ALB)

DK books are available at special discounts when
purchased in bulk for sales promotions, premiums,
fund-raising, or educational use. For details, contact:
DK Publishing Special Markets,
1745 Broadway, 20th Floor, New York, NY 10019
SpecialSales@dk.com

Printed and bound in China

For the curious
www.dk.com

Contents

Amethyst

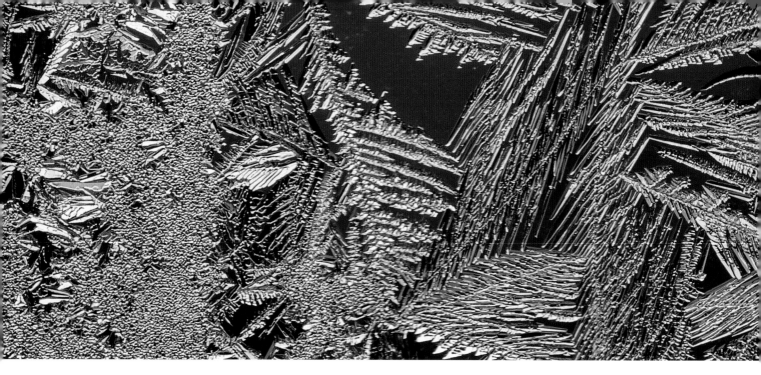

What is a **crystal?**

Associated with perfection, transparency, and clarity (although most are not perfect or transparent), crystals are solid materials with atoms in regular patterns (pp.14–15). Many substances "crystallize," or grow in specific geometric forms with smooth plane surfaces. "Crystal" comes from the Greek word *kryos*, meaning icy—in ancient times, rock crystal was thought to be ice, frozen so hard it would never melt.

Tourmaline crystal

Quartz crystal

Familiar faces

These crystals, formed from hot solutions within Earth, show characteristic faces (flat plane surfaces).

Albite feldspar crystals

Artificial crystal

Most crystals in this book are of natural, solid, inorganic materials called minerals. Some inorganic compounds also form crystals; this potassium magnesium sulphate is an artificially grown crystal.

States of matter

A material, such as water, can exist as a solid, liquid, or gas depending on its temperature. In water vapor, or steam, molecules move around vigorously; in liquid they move slowly; in solid (ice) they form a regular order as a crystalline solid, as shown here.

Massive mineral

Crystals will grow large and perfect in the right conditions. Most, called massive, grow irregularly such as this specimen of the mineral scapolite, with small, poorly formed crystals.

Crystal lining

These fernlike growths, or dendrites (p.21), often found lining rock cracks, look like a plant but are crystalline growths of the mineral pyrolusite.

Cut aquamarine
(pp.38–39)

Cut heliodor
(pp.38–39)

Gem of a crystal

Most gemstones are natural crystals chosen for their beauty, durability, and rarity. They are usually cut and polished (pp.58–59). Crystals can now also be grown artificially (pp.26–27) and cut as gemstones.

Potato surprise

Crystals can occur in unusual places: in plowed fields of south England, irregular nodules known as "potato stones" have sparkling quartz crystals inside.

Mineral-rich water crystallizes to form quartz inside the rock.

Most irregular

Some of the objects we call "crystal" are glass. Glass has little structure, as it is cooled too quickly for the atoms to form a regular order. It is said to be amorphous.

A world of **crystals**

Crystals are all around us. The rocks that form Earth, the Moon, and meteorites (pieces of rock from space) are made up of minerals, most of which are formed of crystals. Earth's three layers—core, mantle, and crust—are made mostly of solid, rock-forming minerals. These minerals are crystalline solids composed of atoms of various elements. We use crystals at home (pp.62–63), at work (pp.28–29), and in technology.

Orthoclase feldspar

Biotite mica

Quartz

Granite
Granite is a characteristic rock of Earth's continental crust (outer layer), made mainly of the minerals quartz, feldspar, and mica. Here, large crystals of the feldspar mineral orthoclase can be seen.

Green pyroxene

Red garnet crystal

Meteorite
The center (core) of Earth may be similarly composed to this iron and nickel meteorite. It has been treated to reveal its crystalline structure.

Eclogite
Earth's upper mantle is probably mostly peridotite and eclogite.

Lava has a temperature of about 1,380°F (1,000°C), making it glow bright orange.

Liquid rock
Runny lava can erupt from volcanoes such as Kilauea, Hawai'i, shown here. When lava cools, minerals crystallize to solid rock.

Strength
Most buildings are made of crystals: rocky materials are mostly crystalline, and their strength depends on the type of rock. Seen here is Rochester Keep, a 12th-century stone castle in Kent, England.

Down to dust

Igneous pebble

Quartzite pebbles

Quartz sand grains

Soil

Pebbles, sand, and soil parts are all formed from weathered and eroded rocks, and will finally be eroded to dust (p.32). All these things are made of crystals.

Drip by drip

Mostly made of calcite crystals, these stalagmites grew in an old mine as water, rich in calcium carbonate, dripped down.

Calcite crystals

Live crystals

The elements that make up most rock-forming minerals are also important to life on Earth. For example, minerals such as calcite and apatite crystallize inside plants and animals.

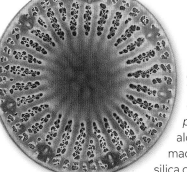

Microcrystals
This microscope diatom, *Cyclotella pseudostelligera*, is algae. Its cell walls are made up of tiny silica crystals.

Human apatite
Bones, such as this human humerus (upper arm bone), contain tiny crystals of the mineral apatite.

Animal mineral
This gallstone from a cow's gallbladder has the same crystalline composition as struvite, a naturally occurring mineral.

Crystal cave
The Naica mine in Mexico has some of the largest natural crystals on Earth, reaching up to 36 ft (11 m) in length. The selenite crystals were formed some 500,000 years ago due to constant high heat from a magma chamber below.

Natural beauty

Well-formed crystals are beautiful and rare. Conditions have to be perfect for them to grow (pp.20–21) and survive, and any changes in conditions must protect, not destroy, them.

Proustite
These cherry-red crystals are known as ruby silvers, and are often found with silver deposits. These are from the silver mine area Chanarcillo, Copiapo, Chile, worked between 1830 and 1880.

Bournonite
These bright-gray "cog-wheel" crystals are from the Herodsfoot lead mine, near Liskeard in Cornwall, England. This mine produced quality bournonite crystals from 1850 to 1875.

Benitoite gems are found **only in San Benito,** California.

Epidote

This is one of the finest epidote crystals known, as it shows fine prismatic habit and color for a crystal of this species. It was found high in the Austrian mountains; the site is said to have been found by a mountain guide in 1865.

EYEWITNESS

Sigalit Landau
Since 2008, Israeli artist Sigalit Landau has sunk objects such as shoes and musical instruments in the very salty waters of the Dead Sea. Salt crystallizes around the objects, which are then taken out, dried, and displayed as works of art.

Topaz

This perfect topaz crystal was one of many found in the 19th century close to the Urulga River, Borshchovochny Mountains, Siberia. Some weighed 22 lb (10 kg).

Epidote is found in metamorphic rocks.

Barite

The iron-mining areas of Cumbria, England, are renowned for their quality barite crystals. The crystals display a range of colors. Each color comes mostly from one mine. These golden-yellow ones are from the Dalmellington mine, Frizington, England.

Red-orange color is due to presence of iron oxide.

Benitoite

These fantastic-quality triangular-shaped, sapphire-blue crystals of benitoite (p.49) were found near the San Benito River, California.

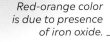

Beautifully formed beryl crystals from various parts of the world

Calcite

A common and widely distributed mineral, calcite crystals occur in many crystal shapes and colors. Some of the most beautiful calcite crystals came from Egremont, Cumbria, England, in the late 19th century. The crystals here are mainly colorless, but some are tinged red.

On the **surface**

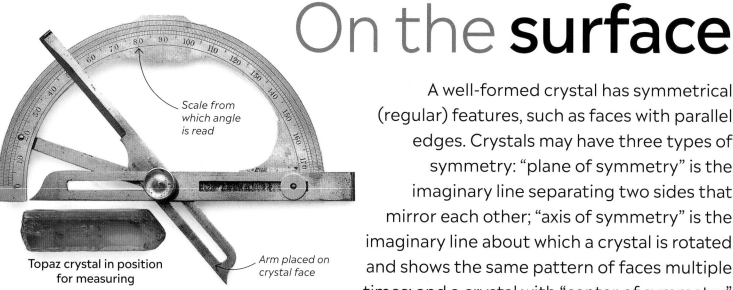

Scale from which angle is read

Arm placed on crystal face

Topaz crystal in position for measuring

A well-formed crystal has symmetrical (regular) features, such as faces with parallel edges. Crystals may have three types of symmetry: "plane of symmetry" is the imaginary line separating two sides that mirror each other; "axis of symmetry" is the imaginary line about which a crystal is rotated and shows the same pattern of faces multiple times; and a crystal with "center of symmetry" is edged by pairs of parallel faces.

Contact goniometer

This measures the angles between crystal faces. The Law of Constancy of Angle states that in all crystals of the same substance, angles of corresponding faces will be the same.

Cubic galena. Symmetry: four threefold axes.

Seven systems

Crystals have differing amounts of symmetry and are classified into one of seven systems. Cubic-system crystals have the highest symmetry, with 9 planes, 12 axes, and a center of symmetry. Triclinic-system crystals have the least symmetry.

Tetragonal vesuvianite. Symmetry: a fourfold axis.

Orthorhombic barite. Symmetry: three twofold axes.

Monoclinic orthoclase (twinned). Symmetry: a twofold axis.

Triclinic axinite. No axis of symmetry.

Same but different

Some crystallographers (crystal researchers) include the trigonal system as part of the hexagonal. Both have the same set of axes, but the trigonal has threefold symmetry.

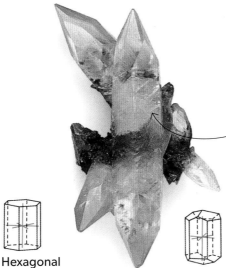

Calcite has the largest number of crystal habits (pp.22-23).

Hexagonal beryl. Symmetry: a sixfold axis.

Trigonal calcite. Symmetry: a threefold axis.

Cubic model

Triclinic model

Hexagonal model

Crystal models

These help crystallographers understand the symmetry. The cotton threads between the faces show axes of rotation.

Form

Crystals of the same mineral may not look alike. The same faces on two crystals may be different sizes and so form different-shaped crystals. Crystals may also vary in "form." Shown here are three forms found in the cubic crystal system, illustrated with pyrite.

Cube form
Each of the six square faces of 90° angles intersects one of the fourfold axes, and is parallel to the other two.

Octahedron form
Each of the eight equilateral triangular faces intersects three of the fourfold axes.

Dodecahedral face

Cubic face

Pyritohedron
This form (also, pentagonal dodecahedron) has 12 five-sided faces.

Octahedral face

CRYSTAL FORMS

Diagram to show the relationship between different cubic forms.

Octahedron

Cube and octahedron

Cube

Cube and pyritohedron

Pyritohedron

Combination of forms
Cubic faces combine with octahedral faces and poorly developed dodecahedral faces.

Inside **crystals**

A crystal's properties, such as regular shape, are decided by its internal structure of atoms. Each atom has a set place, tied to others by bonds. The atoms of a mineral always group the same way to form its crystals. One of the first to see an inner regularity was Abbé Hauy, in 1784. With Röntgen's X-ray discovery in 1895, Max von Laue realized X-rays could be used to see atomic structure.

Graphite

Graphite

Graphite's carbon atoms are linked in a hexagonal way in widely spaced layers. The weak bonds between the layers make it a soft mineral.

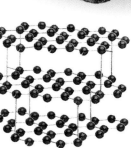

Structural model of graphite

Diamond crystal

Structural model of diamond

Diamond

Each carbon atom is strongly bonded to four others. This makes diamond very hard.

Augite crystal

Oxygen atom *Silicon atom*

Tetrahedra double-chain silicate

Augite

Augite is one of an important group of silicates, the pyroxenes, with a structure based on one chain of SiO_4 tetrahedra.

Model showing SiO_4 tetrahedra in a single-chain silicate

Actinolite

Silicate minerals, in all common rocks except limestone, have a tetrahedron makeup: one silicon and four oxygen atoms (SiO_4). Actinolite's structure is based on a double chain of tetrahedra.

ELECTROMAGNETIC WAVES

X-rays are part of the electromagnetic radiation spectrum. All radiations can be described in terms of waves, such as light, radio, and heat. The waves differ in length and frequency. White light, visible to the human eye, is electromagnetic waves varying in length between red and violet in the spectrum (p.16).

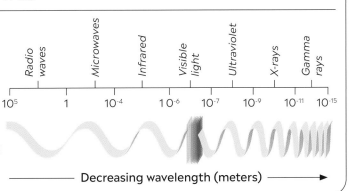

Radio waves | Microwaves | Infrared | Visible light | Ultraviolet | X-rays | Gamma rays

10^5 | 1 | 10^{-4} | 10^{-6} | 10^{-7} | 10^{-9} | 10^{-11} | 10^{-15}

← Decreasing wavelength (meters) →

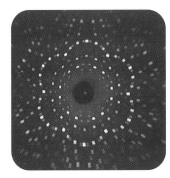

X-ray photo

In 1912, German physicist Max von Laue took X-ray photos of atoms in crystals. The photo above shows the symmetrical pattern in beryl, related to the hexagonal symmetry of the crystal.

Beryl

Beryl (pp.38–39) and other silicate minerals' internal structure has groups of six tetrahedra, linked in rings.

Cleavage

Some crystals split along planes called cleavage planes, which are the same for all crystals of a species. They form along the structure's weakest planes and are proof of the orderly lineup of atoms.

Thin cleavage flakes

Micas
In this group of silicates, the atom bonds at 90° to its "sheet structure" are weak. Cleavage occurs easily along these planes.

Cleavage plane

Quartz
Quartz structure is based on a strongly bonded network of silicon and oxygen atoms. Crystals do not split easily but show a smooth, curved fracture known as conchoidal.

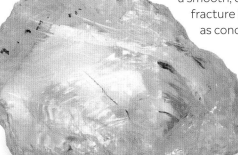

Topaz
This blue topaz crystal from Madagascar has a perfect cleavage. Topaz has isolated SiO_4 groups in its structure.

Crystal color

Crystal color can be striking. Something looks a specific color as your eye and brain react to light wavelengths (p.15). When white light (daylight) falls on a crystal, some wavelengths may be reflected, some absorbed. If some are absorbed, you see a color other than white because some of the white light wavelengths are missing.

Opaque, milky quartz

Transparent, colorless rock crystal

Rock crystal can be used to make lenses or prisms.

Translucent, purple amethyst

Transparent or opaque

Crystals can be transparent (see through, letting nearly all light through), translucent (letting some light through), or opaque (are not see through, letting no light through).

Sulfur crystals are brittle and odorless.

Idiochromatic

Idiochromatic minerals are nearly always the same color because certain light-absorbing atoms are an essential part of their crystal structure.

Sulfur
This idiochromatic mineral normally crystallizes in bright yellow crystals, often found near volcanic vents (p.20).

Ancient Chinese people discovered how to make gunpowder from sulfur.

Azurite formed on a groundmass of geothite, a form of iron hydroxide.

Azurite
This copper mineral is always blue—hence the term azure blue. It was used as a pigment in ancient times.

Rounded crystal shape

Allochromatic

Some minerals are allochromatic—they are a range of colors due to impurities or light-absorbing defects in the atomic structure. For example, quartz and diamond can be red, green, yellow, and blue.

Rhodochrosite

Manganese minerals such as this are usually pink or red. Rare red beryls are bright red due to small amounts of manganese.

A thin crust of erythrite on a brown rock base.

Fluorite

Some minerals are fluorescent—they are various colors in ultraviolet (UV) light (p.15). This is usually caused by foreign atoms (activators) in the crystal structure. This fluorite crystal is blue in UV light, but green in daylight.

Erythrite

Cobalt minerals are usually pink or reddish. Trace amounts of cobalt may color colorless minerals.

Play of colors

Some minerals have a play of colors, like that in an oil film or soap bubble. This may be produced when the light is affected by the physical structure of the crystals, such as twinning (p.21), cleavage planes (p.15), or by the development during growth of thin films. Microscopic intergrowths of platelike inclusions (p.21) also cause light interference.

Salt

A missing atom in a crystal's structure can form a color center. Coloration of common salt is thought to be caused by this.

Labradorite

This feldspar mineral often forms dull gray crystalline masses. Internal twinning causes interference of light, which gives the mineral a sheen, or schiller, with patches of different colors.

Crystals arranged in "iron rose" formation

Hematite

The play of colors on these crystals is called iridescence. It is due to the interference of light in thin surface films.

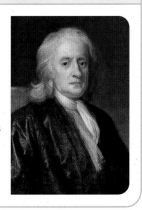

Identification

To identify a crystal, its properties must be tested. Color (pp.16–17), habit (pp.22–23), cleavage (p.15), and surface features can be studied using a hand lens. Others, such as hardness and specific gravity (SG), require basic equipment. Sophisticated instruments are needed to test for atomic structure and chemical composition.

Orthoclase SG = 2.6   Galena SG = 7.4

Specific gravity

An important property, SG is the ratio of a substance's weight compared to that of an equal volume of water. These crystals are similar in size but their SG is different, reflecting the atoms' mass and how they are packed together.

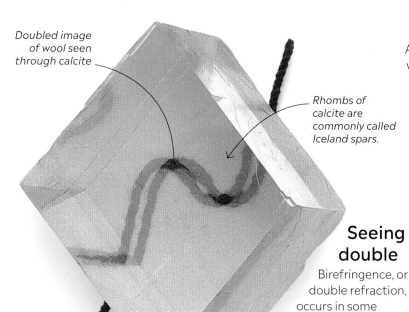

Doubled image of wool seen through calcite

Rhombs of calcite are commonly called Iceland spars.

Seeing double

Birefringence, or double refraction, occurs in some crystals. In this rhomb of calcite, light is split into two rays, causing a doubled image.

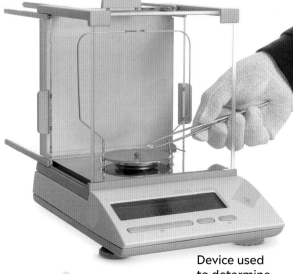

Device used to determine specific gravity

Hardness

The property of hardness depends on the strength of the forces holding a solid's atoms together. In 1812, Friedrich Mohs devised a scale of hardness, using 10 minerals. Each can scratch only those below it on the scale. Intervals of hardness are roughly equal except for between corundum (9) and diamond (10).

1
Talc

2
Gypsum

3
Calcite

4
Fluorite

Probing around

Electron probe microanalysis was used to investigate the specimen (left). In a scanning electron microscope (SEM), a beam of electrons was focused on the specimen, producing an X-ray spectrum (below).

Images from the microscope are seen on the screen.

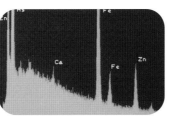

The X-ray spectrum showing large peaks for iron (Fe), arsenic (As), calcium (Ca), and zinc (Zn)

Ruby, colored by chromium

Almandine garnet, colored by iron

Absorbed in stone

A spectroscope can distinguish between similarly colored gems. It shows dark bands on the spectrum where wavelengths have been absorbed by the gem.

Mistaken identity

Modern techniques can better reveal chemical composition. X-rays showed these small, blue-gray crystals on limonite to be the mineral symplesite (hydrated iron arsenate). But further analysis showed some unexpected calcium and zinc, too.

Shadow play

Refractive index (RI) measures, using a refractometer, how well a mineral bends light. It is useful in identification. The position of one or two shadow edges from light passing through the stone gives the RI.

Spinel
RI: 1.71

Tourmaline
RI: 1.62 and 1.64

10
Diamond

9
Corundum

8
Topaz

7
Quartz

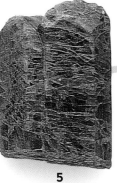

5
Apatite

6
Orthoclase

Natural growth

Crystals grow as atoms arrange themselves in a regular network (pp.14–15), layer by layer. Growth continues by adding material to the outer surfaces. Temperature, pressure, chemical conditions, and space all affect growth. In an hour, millions of atoms arrange themselves across a crystal face. With this number, it is not surprising defects occur—a perfect crystal is rare.

Mineral springs

Hot, watery solutions and gases containing minerals, such as sal ammoniac, reach Earth's surface in hot springs or gas vents. Here, the minerals may crystallize.

Sal ammoniac crystals

Twisted

Crystals can be bent, like this stibnite, perhaps due to mechanical bending as it grew.

Settling down

As magma cools, crystals of various minerals form. Some build up in layers, as different minerals settle and crystallize at varying times.

Changed by force

These blue kyanite and brown staurolite crystals were formed by metamorphism: high temperatures and pressures in Earth's crust cause minerals to recrystallize, forming new minerals.

Taking shape

Many minerals crystallize from watery solutions, which reveals their formation sequence. Here, a fluorite crystal grew, was coated with siderite, but then dissolved. The siderite coating kept fluorite's cubic shape. Lastly, quartz and chalcopyrite crystals grew in the cube.

Quartz

Siderite

Chalcopyrite

Spiraling around

Crystal faces are rarely flat, due to growth defects. This magnified image of indium antimonite crystals shows a continuous spiral instead of layers across the crystal face.

Beryl etching

Solutions or hot gases may dissolve crystal surfaces (left) forming regularly shaped hollows, or etch pits. Their shape reflects atomic structure.

Fluid inclusion

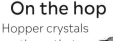

"Phantom" growth layers

Crystal enclosure

During growth, a crystal may enclose fluids or crystals of other minerals. These are known as inclusions.

Fluorite crystal with inclusions

On the hop

Hopper crystals are those that build up quicker along face edges, like these galena crystals, than at the centers. This produces cavities in the faces.

Phantom quartz

Interruptions in a crystal's growth can produce regular inclusions. Parallel growth layers ("phantoms"), as in this quartz, formed as dark-green chlorite coated the crystal as it grew.

Twinning

During crystallization, two crystals of the same mineral may develop to be joined at a common plane. These are known as twinned crystals. The contact between the two parts is the twin plane.

Butterfly twins

This calcite shows a butterfly contact twin crystal, named after its likeness to butterfly wings.

Striations on pyrite crystal

Growing up together

When the two parts of twin crystals are intergrown, they are called penetration twins.

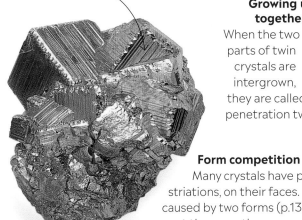

Form competition

Many crystals have parallel lines, or striations, on their faces. These can be caused by two forms (p.13) trying to grow at the same time.

Crystal habits

A crystal's shape is called its habit. It is important in crystallography and is very useful in identification. The forms (p.13) or group of forms that a crystal develops are often what give it a particular habit. As crystals grow, some faces develop more than others and their relative sizes create different shapes. Most minerals occur in groups and rarely show fine crystal shapes. These are aggregates.

Tabular
This large red crystal of wulfenite is from the Red Cloud mine, Arizona. Its habit is tabular.

Acicular
The radiating, slender mesolite crystals in this aggregate are acicular (needlelike). They are very fragile and can pierce skin. This group is from Mumbai, India.

Stalactitic
These aggregates of goethite are stalactitic. Goethite is an important iron ore. This group is from Coblenz, Rhineland, Germany.

Giant's Causeway
This formation in County Antrim, Northern Ireland, looks like hexagonal crystals but has joints from contraction as basalt lava cooled.

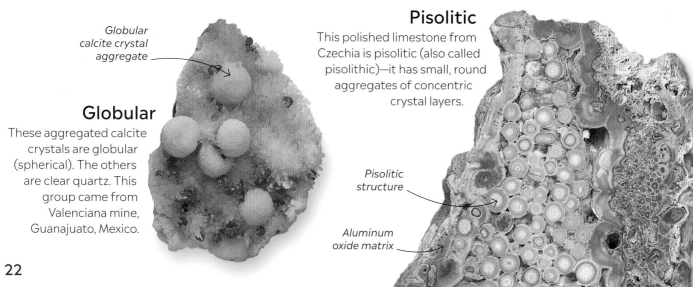

Pisolitic
This polished limestone from Czechia is pisolitic (also called pisolithic)—it has small, round aggregates of concentric crystal layers.

Globular calcite crystal aggregate

Globular
These aggregated calcite crystals are globular (spherical). The others are clear quartz. This group came from Valenciana mine, Guanajuato, Mexico.

Pisolitic structure

Aluminum oxide matrix

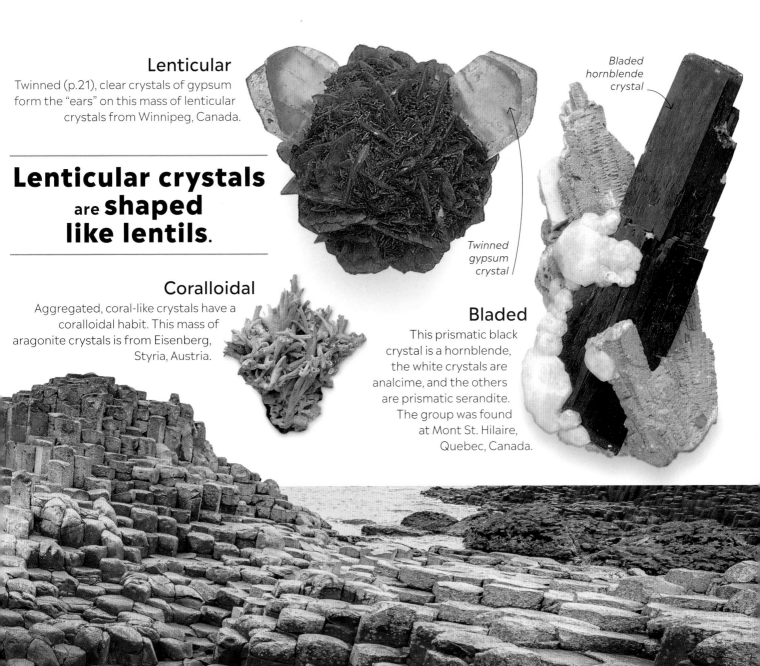

Lenticular
Twinned (p.21), clear crystals of gypsum form the "ears" on this mass of lenticular crystals from Winnipeg, Canada.

Lenticular crystals are shaped like lentils.

Bladed hornblende crystal

Twinned gypsum crystal

Coralloidal
Aggregated, coral-like crystals have a coralloidal habit. This mass of aragonite crystals is from Eisenberg, Styria, Austria.

Bladed
This prismatic black crystal is a hornblende, the white crystals are analcime, and the others are prismatic serandite. The group was found at Mont St. Hilaire, Quebec, Canada.

Dendritic
Dendritic, meaning treelike, describes the habit of these copper crystals from Broken Hill, New South Wales, Australia. Copper often forms in hydrothermal deposits, but is also found as grains in sandstones.

Two forms
The calcite crystal "mushrooms" (right) show two forms: a scalenohedron forms the "stem" topped by a rhombohedron.

Massive
Crystals that grow in a mass, where individual crystals cannot be clearly seen, are called massive. Dumortierite is a rare mineral. It is usually massive, like this piece from Bahia, Brazil.

Extraction

Humans have searched for mineral deposits since prehistoric times. Some, such as copper, occur in great quantity; others like gold and diamond occur in smaller quantities but are sold at higher prices. Profitable mining requires large quantities in one area and easy extraction by quarrying, panning and dredging, or deep mining. Minerals from which useful metals are extracted are called ores.

Scattered grains

Open-pit quarrying works rocks of just one percent ore. The ore, like this chalcopyrite copper ore, occurs as small grains, but the whole rock has to be worked. A huge hole and lots of gangue (waste) is produced.

Liroconite crystals from a secondary enriched layer

Vein of covellite, a copper sulphide, from a secondary sulphide enrichment layer

Chalcopyrite copper ore

Quartz

Gradual improvement

Groundwaters filter down through rock and carry elements downward, redepositing them in a rock's lower layers. This enrichment improves low-grade ores to higher concentrations. These enriched layers in copper deposits may contain azurite and liroconite, or sulphide minerals, such as bornite and chalcocite.

Rich vein

Larger amounts of ore occur in veins, but most high-grade ores have been found and worked out by deep mining. This vein has quartz and chalcopyrite in altered granite.

On the surface

Russia is the world's largest producer of diamonds. Seen here is the open pit of the Mirny mine, Russia, with a depth of 1,722 ft (525 m). The massive depth causes it to have drastically different temperatures and airflows than surrounding areas.

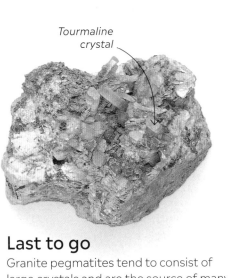

Tourmaline crystal

Swirling waters

Panning is a simple way of separating minerals, often used to sort gem-rich river gravels in areas such as Myanmar (Burma) and Thailand. Swirling water in a pan washes away less dense gangue minerals, leaving wanted minerals behind.

Last to go

Granite pegmatites tend to consist of large crystals and are the source of many fine gems, formed by the slow cooling and crystallization of the last fluids left after most of the granite has solidified.

Traditional gold panning in Thailand

Gem deposits mixed with gravel

Down under

Much mining takes place underground, as at the Mirny mine in eastern Russia.

Smaller than some

These beryl crystals measure about 8 x 5.5 in (20 x 14 cm), but are small compared to some crystals in pegmatites.

Growing
crystals

Scientists have manufactured crystals for more than a century. Naturally grown crystals are flawed (pp.20–21); synthetic ones can be made flawless, and to grow to a specific shape and size. Artificial crystals are vital to modern technology. Grown crystals are used in almost every electronic or optical device. Developments in electronics depend mainly on the development of crystal-growing techniques.

In a flux

Many emeralds are produced by flux fusion: a powder of emerald ingredients is heated with a flux (solid). The flux melts and the powder dissolves. It is then left to cool and forms crystals over several months.

Synthetic emerald crystal

Cut synthetic emerald

Drawn out

Pure silicon does not occur naturally, so crystals are made. Quartz sand heated with coke produces nearly pure silicon. In one process, a seed crystal on a rotating rod is dipped into the melt and slowly removed, which is called "drawing a crystal."

Melt technique

Excellent crystals may be grown by slow cooling or evaporation of a supersaturated solution (no more will dissolve) of a salt like halite, alum, or ammonium dihydrogen phosphate (ADP). In this experiment, powdered ADP with a small chrome-alum impurity has dissolved in boiling water and then cooled.

Transparent ADP crystals

Supersaturated solution

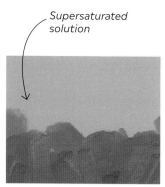

Liquid cools rapidly. Stubby but cloudy prismatic crystals form.

Crystals grow slowly, allowing them to become clearer.

At room temperature, crystals grow slowly due to evaporation.

Cooling stops, but evaporation continues. Crystals slowly grow.

Synthetic sapphire boule

Two halves of synthetic ruby boule

Hexagonal carborundum crystal

Flame fusion

August Verneuil was the first to commercially produce synthetic ruby. He achieved this in 1902, using the flame fusion method. Powdered material fed through a flame fuses into liquid and drips on a support. Pulling the support from the heat forms a crystal, or boule.

Support for growing crystal

Synthetic rubies produced in a crucible

Grown in size

In 1877, French chemist Fremy was the first to grow well-sized gem-quality crystals. In 2020, Dale Vince founded Skydiamond, which uses carbon from the air to create synthetic diamonds from sustainable sources.

Skydiamond facility in UK

Henri Moisson
While studying meteorite fragments, French chemist Henri Moisson (1852–1907) found a new natural silicon carbide mineral in 1893. It was named moissonite after him. A synthetic form of moissonite is used to make gemstones that imitate diamonds.

Abrasive character

Silicon carbide is nearly as hard as diamond. It has many uses, including being used as an abrasive called carborundum that is produced in electrically fired furnaces. Silicon carbide is also grown as large crystals and used as a synthetic gemstone called moissonite.

Crystals at work

Crystals play an important part in this age of rapid technological change. They are used in control circuits, machines, electronics, communications, industrial tools, medicine, and credit cards. New crystals for new purposes are being developed. From the crystal laboratory (pp.26–27) have already come ruby laser rods, silicon chips, and diamonds for tools.

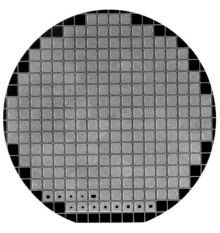

Silicon slice
Silicon chips are made from wafers (thin slices) cut from artificial crystals of pure silicon (p.26). The wafers are etched with electronic circuits, which are transferred to the wafer from a matrix (piece of film).

Circuits
Many different chips are needed in a computer. Each chip has a different circuit to run a specific part. Every chip is protected in a case, then linked to others on a circuit board.

The **Pioneer Venus probe** had a diamond window that could **withstand Venus's** temperature of 840°F (450°C).

Smart cards
There is a tiny computer on a silicon chip in every "smart card." The chip contains information about the user that can be read by a scanner. Smart cards are used for credit cards, driving licenses, identity cards, and transit tickets.

Ruby rod
Synthetic ruby crystals are used to make a beam of pure red laser light. Their heated atoms are stimulated by light to emit radiation waves.

LASERS

Laser beams can be focused to tiny points generating intense heat, put to use in welding, drilling, and surgery. In a ruby laser, light from a lamp makes a ruby rod emit radiation, which is focused by mirrors at the ends. The focused light then comes out as a laser beam.

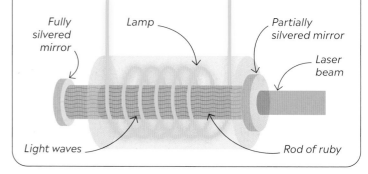

Fully silvered mirror

Lamp

Partially silvered mirror

Laser beam

Light waves

Rod of ruby

Diamond tools

Diamonds are widely used, in sawing, drilling, grinding, and polishing—from quarrying stone to delicate eye surgery—mainly because they are so hard. They come in a range of sizes, shapes, and strengths. More than 80 percent of industrial diamonds are synthetic.

Drill bits

Diamond-tipped drill bits are used for drilling all types of rock, such as in drilling oil wells. The diamonds are different shapes for different uses. Some contain diamonds set in the surface; others are impregnated with tiny pieces of diamond grit.

Drill bit containing surface-set natural diamonds

Cutting segment containing synthetic diamond grit

Drill bit impregnated with synthetic diamond grit

Saw blade

Diamond-set saws are used for cutting glass, ceramics, and rocks. The blades have industrial diamonds in a "carrier" such as brass, bonded to a steel disc. The carrier wears away to expose new diamonds.

A surgeon using a diamond-bladed scalpel in delicate eye surgery

Diamond blade

Diamond grit

Grit and powders, used for polishing and grinding, are mainly made from synthetic diamonds.

Diamond scalpel

As well as being hard, diamond does not corrode. This is one reason diamonds are used in surgery.

Diamond wire

Cutting with a diamond wire reduces material loss. The wire can be used around a drum or as a continuous loop.

"Bead" containing synthetic diamond abrasive

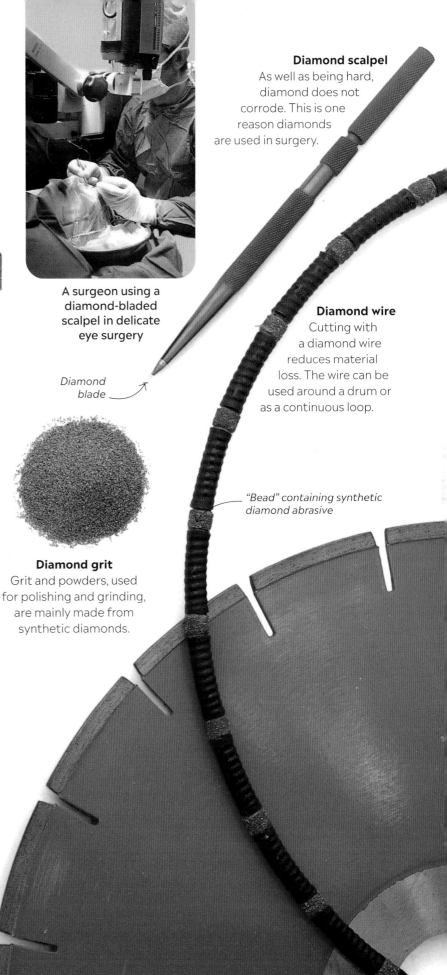

Crystal vibrations

Quartz is a common mineral. It is widely found as veins (p.24) and with other mineral deposits, and is a main constituent of granite, sandstones, and sand. As quartzite and sandstone, it is used for building and manufacturing glass. Its crystals have a piezoelectric effect, and quartz is used to make crystal oscillators that form part of electronic circuits for communication systems such as television and radio.

Waves of energy

Quartz crystals are used in electronics. They can change a mechanical force, such as a blow from a hammer, into electrical energy.

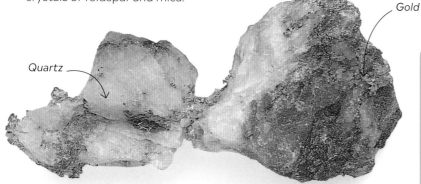

Quartz

Mica

Feldspar

Crystal trio

Crystals of quartz can be seen in this granite pegmatite crystal group (p.25), along with crystals of feldspar and mica.

Six-sided prismatic crystal

English prism

Quartz commonly crystallizes as six-sided prisms with rhombohedral ends (pp.12–13). The prism axis shows only threefold symmetry. On many crystals, alternate faces show different growth patterns.

Gold

Quartz

Going for gold

Many quartz veins carry metallic mineral deposits (p.24). This specimen, from the British gold extraction site at St. David's mine, Wales, contains gold. In mining, the quartz would be considered as gangue (unwanted mineral).

👁 EYEWITNESS

Issac Koga

In 1933, Japanese scientist Issac Koga invented synthetic quartz crystal plates that are not sensitive to changes in temperature and oscillate at a stable frequency. These plates are used in wireless communications systems, which require stable frequencies to operate.

Small face showing left-handedness

Right-handed quartz crystal

Ambidextrous

In quartz crystals, silicon and oxygen atoms are joined in a tetrahedron (four-sided triangular pyramid). Linked in spirals, they can be left- or right-handed. This structure accounts for quartz piezoelectricity.

Left-handed quartz crystal

The brown hue is due to exposure to underground radiation.

Crystal clear

Crystals from groups, like this one from Arkansas, are prized for their beauty and clarity, and may be used in crystal healing therapies.

A crystal therapy session

Crystal pendant thought by some to help with healing

Alpine architecture

This "twisted" group of smoky quartz crystals shows some beautiful crystal "architecture." Such crystal groups are often found in the Alps in Europe.

Piezoelectricity

In 1880, Pierre and Jacques Curie discovered that pressure on a quartz crystal causes positive and negative charges across it—piezoelectricity. It was later found that alternating electrical charges cause a piezoelectric crystal to vibrate—the basis for quartz to be used as oscillators to control radio waves, or keep time.

Jacques and Pierre Curie with their parents

Pure necessity
Synthetic crystals like this are grown by a hydrothermal process (p.26) to make oscillator plates.

Watch piece
This micro-thin quartz crystal slice is used to keep time in a quartz watch.

Quartz crystal slice

Split-second timing
The crystal slice in a watch vibrates more than 30,000 times per second, making it a good timekeeper.

Quartz

Quartz is silicon dioxide. It occurs as crystals and fine-grained masses (called jaspers or chalcedonies) in many forms, patterns, and colors. In the right conditions, giant crystals can grow—one of the largest recorded single crystals was more than 20 ft (6 m) long and weighed more than 52.8 tons (48 metric tons). Quartz is tough with no cleavage (p.15), making it ideal for carving and cutting; it is widely used as a gem.

Dunes and dust
Quartz forms quartz sand dunes and some dust. The dust can damage gems of 6 or less on Mohs' hardness scale.

Quartz crystal
Crystal system: trigonal; hardness: 7; specific gravity: 2.65.

Single crystals
Single crystals of quartz include amethyst, rose and smoky quartz, colorless rock crystal, and yellow citrine. They're often big enough to be cut as gems.

Impure of heart
Colorless rock crystal is the purest form of quartz. The many other colors are caused by impurities. Amethyst and citrine, for example, contain iron.

Amethyst
This is the most common form of quartz. Crystals occur in granite veins in the Ural Mountains, Russia, and in basalt cavities in Brazil, Uruguay, and India.

Rose quartz
Single crystals are rare. Most rose quartz is massive, best cut as cabochons (p.59). Some can be polished to display a star.

Jasper
Interlocking microcrystalline quartz and jasper are mixed in with colorful impurities that give it different colors. Shown here is Jasper Creek, Venezuela, where water flows over a bed of red and black jasper.

Massive

There are several massive varieties of quartz, made of tiny grains or fibers. Chalcedony—such as carnelian, chrysoprase, and agate—and jasper are distinguished by their grain patterns. Tiger's-eye and hawk's-eye form when asbestos is replaced by quartz and iron oxides.

Amethyst

Agate

Garnet

Pearl

Citrine

Amazonite

Aquamarine

Agate

Rare beauty
This 19th-century gold box is set with a superb rare citrine surrounded by a stunning variety of other gems.

Rock crystal

Vein of carnelian

Agate
Quartz grains in chalcedony occur in layers. Here, they progressively crystallized inward in a lava cavity.

Entry point of quartz solution into lava cavity

Carnelian
Most specimens of this translucent orange-red chalcedony result from heat-treating a less attractive chalcedony. This turns iron-bearing minerals into iron oxides, giving orange-red colors.

Bands of agate

Polished tiger's-eye showing the eye effect called chatoyancy

Chrysoprase
At its finest, chrysoprase is a vibrant green and a valuable chalcedony. It has been used in ornaments and decorative patterns since prehistoric times.

Diamond

Derived from the Greek word *adamas* meaning "unconquerable," diamond is so called because of its supreme hardness. Made of pure carbon with an immensely strong crystal structure (p.14), evidence suggests that diamonds were formed about 125 miles (200 km) deep within Earth. Discovered more than 2,000 years ago from river gravels in India, diamonds are now mined in more than 20 countries—Russia supplies a third of the world's needs. A brilliant cut (p.58) best reveals its luster and fire.

Diamond

Volcanic gemstone

This diamond is embedded in kimberlite, a volcanic rock first discovered in Kimberley, South Africa.

Diamond crystal

Crystal system: cubic; hardness: 10; specific gravity: 3.5.

Rough diamonds

Rough diamonds mined from kimberlites often have lustrous crystal faces. Those from gravels can be dull due to being carried along in rough water with other rocks.

Alluvial diamonds

Mined diamonds

Diamond rush

In 1866, a diamond was found close to Hopetown, South Africa, with a larger one—the Star of Africa—found in 1869. This sparked the South African Diamond Rush, with prospectors from around the world coming to South Africa hoping to find a fortune in diamonds.

Rich mix

Conglomerate rock is a cemented mixture of rounded pebbles and mineral grains from water deposits. This South African specimen is rich in diamonds.

Unconquerable

Napoleon Bonaparte's sword was set with the Regent diamond. He hoped it would bring victory in battle, from the ancient belief that a diamond made its wearer unconquerable.

Embedded diamond

Brilliant colors

Most natural diamonds are near-colorless; truly colorless ones are rare. A few are all colors in the spectrum; good-quality ones are "fancies."

Butterfly brooch

This brooch is set with more than 150 diamonds.

Indian diamond

Embedded in a sandy conglomerate, this rough diamond is from Hyderabad, India—the source of many famous large diamonds.

Diamonds are a girl's best friend

This song is from *Gentlemen Prefer Blondes*, in which Marilyn Monroe wore a yellow diamond called the Moon of Baroda.

Murchison snuffbox

Set with diamonds and a portrait of Tsar Alexander II of Russia, this gold box was presented to Sir Roderick Murchison in 1867 in recognition of his geological work in Russia.

The diamonds on the box range from 0.75 to 2.5 carats.

Famous diamonds

Some exceptional diamonds have long histories, and others have inspired fantastic legends.

The jewel in the crown

The Koh-i-noor (mountain of light) is said to be the oldest large diamond, found in India. Initially owned by Mughal kings, it was presented to Queen Victoria in 1850. Its cut (above) was unimpressive, so it was recut (p.58).

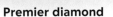

Premier diamond

In 1905, the Cullinan crystal (actual size shown here) was mined in the Transvaal, South Africa, weighing 3,106 carats—the largest diamond ever found. In 1908, it was cut into smaller stones.

Blue Hope

The 45.52-carat blue Hope is famed for bringing bad luck. It is now in the Smithsonian Institution. Its blue color is due to the presence of trace amounts of boron.

Corundum

Corundum is an aluminum oxide, next to diamond in hardness, and is pleochroic (the color varies from different sides). Ruby and sapphire are varieties. Only true red stones are rubies, and sapphire indicates a blue stone, although other colors are called sapphire, such as pink sapphire. Most gems are found in gravels; the most famous are in Sri Lanka, Myanmar (Burma), and Kashmir.

Corundum
Crystal system: trigonal; hardness: 9; specific gravity: 3.96–4.05.

Twin sapphire crystals

Sapphire intergrown with tourmaline

Kashmir blue
Kashmir has a reputation for sapphires of the finest blue. The term Kashmir blue describes sapphires of this color from elsewhere, too.

In a spinel
Sapphires are often found with spinels in gem gravels, but rarely in their source rock. This Myanmar sapphire grew with spinel crystals under high temperature and pressure.

Myanmar crystal
Most quality rubies come from the Mogok region in Myanmar (Burma). Rubies from Myanmar, Pakistan, and Afghanistan are often found in calcite.

Rich colors
Pure corundum is colorless. Impurities are the cause of colors: chromium (red), iron (yellow and green), and iron and titanium (blue).

Bazaar dealing

This 2015 photograph shows ruby dealers in a Mogok bazaar in Myanmar (Burma). Gem-quality corundum is rare; ruby is the most valuable, fetching higher prices than diamonds of a similar size.

Queen cameo

These gems, mounted on a large crystal jug in about 1660, with a ruby cameo of English queen Elizabeth I, were only rediscovered in 1985.

Star ruby

Some rubies display stars from fine needlelike inclusions (p.21) of rutile, such as the 138.7-carat Rosser Reeves ruby. It belongs to the Smithsonian Institution.

Blue sapphire pin of Buddha

Citrine

Zircon

Sapphire

Sapphire

Gem-set

This silver cross is set with six sapphires, an inky-blue spinel, citrine, amethyst, and a brown zircon, with another sapphire at the top.

Hard as rock

Most natural corundum is not gem quality. It is opaque, and gray or brown like this crystal from Madagascar. This hard material is used in industrial tools.

Abrasive rock

Emery, like this fine-grained rock from Ikaria, Greece, is impure corundum. Intergrown with black hematite and magnetite, it is typical of rocks used as abrasives.

Peacock throne

Gem expert Shah Jahan reigned over India from 1627–1658. His Peacock Throne was set with hundreds of gems, including 108 rubies.

Beryl

Popular for its resistance to wear and its fine colors, beryl includes emerald (green), aquamarine (blue green), heliodor (yellow), and morganite (pink). Beryl is found in pegmatites (p.25) and granites. In its non-gem form, crystals can weigh as much as the 60 ft-(18 m-) long Madagascan record holder at 39.6 tons (36 metric tons).

Beryl crystal

Crystal system: hexagonal; hardness: 7.5; specific gravity 2.63–2.91.

Crown of the Andes

The Chibcha people of Colombia mined emeralds, which, through trade, reached the Incas in Peru and Aztecs in Mexico. In the early 1500s, the Spanish wanted to find their source, but did not find the Chivor mine until 1537. Looted Incan and Aztec artifacts were melted down and used to make Spanish treasures, such as the Crown of the Andes (right).

Russian host

A typical source of emeralds is mica schist. It was found in the early 1800s in the Ural mountains, Russia.

Emerald crystal embedded in white calcite

Geologist with an emerald at Muzo mine, Colombia

Mined for life

The world's finest emeralds come from around Muzo and Chivor, Colombia. Many are mined and exported illegally.

Ancient mine

Emeralds were mined near the Red Sea in Egypt from 1500 BCE. The mines were rediscovered in 1816 but were not profitable. This old entrance was discovered in about 1900.

Fine cut

This 911-carat, fine cut aquamarine is owned by the Smithsonian Institution.

Second-class crystal

A few emeralds are still found in Egypt in areas of granite, schist, and serpentine. Most crystals are bluish green with many inclusions.

Dry red

Red beryl is extremely rare. It occurs in "dry" rhyolite volcanic rocks, mainly in Utah and Montana, and Mexico. Red beryl has also been found in Madagascar and Afghanistan.

Color causes

Pure beryl is colorless. The reds and pinks are caused by manganese, the blues and yellows by iron, the emerald green by chromium and vanadium.

Sea green

Aquamarine means seawater and describes its color, caused by varying amounts of iron forms. It is fairly common, and its main source is in Brazil.

Morganite

Tourmaline inclusions

Heliodor

The emeralds on the hilt are not cut but polished.

Gem belts

This large, gem-quality beryl crystal from Brazil is made up of zones of the varieties morganite and heliodor.

Turkish delight

The Topkapi Palace Treasury in Istanbul, Türkiye (Turkey), contains many pieces with fine emeralds, such as in the hilt of this 18th-century dagger.

Opal

Opal
Crystal system: amorphous; hardness: 5.5–6.5; specific gravity: 1.98–2.25.

Non-flashy
Nonprecious opal without flashes of color is called potch. Rose opal is potch, but it is popular for decorative jewelry. This specimen comes from France; other sources are in Idaho.

The ancient Romans used opal as a symbol of power, but at times it has been considered unlucky. The Aztecs mined opal more than 500 years ago in Central America, which is still an important source, mainly of fire opal. The top producer of black and white opal is Australia. Opal is one of the few noncrystalline gems, with a tendency to crack and chip.

The plague of Venice
During the Black Death, depicted here by Antonio Zanchi, Venetians found opals unlucky—they brightened when a wearer caught the disease and dulled when they died.

Flash of lightning
The finest black opal is from Lightning Ridge, New South Wales, Australia. The color flashes are dramatic against its dark body, which, coupled with its rarity, makes it more valuable than white opal.

Glassy look
This clear, glassy looking opal (hyalite) from Czechia occurs in volcanic-lava cavities. Those with a play of color are the prized water opal. Hydrophane is opaque but appears colorless in water.

Greatly enlarged photograph of precious opal, showing the ordered silica spheres

Australian fair

The major Australian opal deposits occur in sedimentary rocks in the Great Artesian Basin. Famous mines include White Cliffs, Lightning Ridge, and Coober Pedy. The Coober Pedy region produces 70 percent of the world's opal.

Flashing lights

Precious opal has flashes of color, dependent on its structural silica-sphere sizes. Opal with a dark background is called black; others, white.

On the map

"Prospector's brooches" in the shape of Australia marked the arrival on the market in the late 1800s of Australian opal.

Moved in

The opal localities in Australia are very hot. When mines are worked out, the near-surface excavations are adapted into cool living spaces.

Mexican fire

Mexico is famous for its fire opal—a nearly transparent variety, showing flashes of color. It ranges from yellow to orange and red.

Potch opal

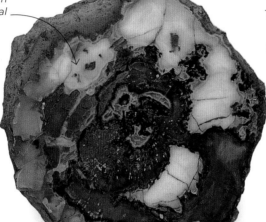

Boulder opal

If this hardened sandy clay with iron oxides and precious-opal layers has enough iron, it gives the rock a dark color. Its flat opal surfaces can be carved into cameos.

An Australian black opal in matrix

Precious fossil

Opal often replaces bones and shells of animals, plus wood tissue, as in this wood from Nevada. It grows bit by bit to replace the original material in fossils.

Pineapple opal

This was an aggregate of radiating crystals of glauberite but it has been replaced by precious opal. Found in Australia, this type of opal is popularly known as "pineapple opal."

Other gemstones

A gemstone's properties are said to be beauty, rarity, and durability. As well as those detailed on previous pages, gems that adorn jewelers' shops include topaz, tourmaline, garnet, and peridot. Some such as kunzite, sphene, and fluorite are too soft or rare, and are cut only for collectors.

Marvelous gems
Japanese pearl diving is a centuries-old tradition. Female divers are known as *ama* (sea women).

Topaz crystal
Crystal system: orthorhombic; hardness: 8; specific gravity: 3.52–3.56.

Topaz
The history of topaz, before it was named in the early 18th century, is unclear. Its name is said to come from *Topazius*, Greek for Zabargad—an island in the Red Sea.

Crystal fame
This pale-blue crystal is from Brazil—the most famous topaz source. Other sources include the US, Japan, and Russia.

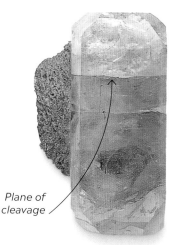

Plane of cleavage

Needs protection
Although very hard, topaz can be easily broken because it has one direction of perfect cleavage (p.15), seen clearly in this crystal. Any jewelry setting for topaz must therefore protect the gemstone.

One of the best
The best golden topaz is from Ouro Prêto, Brazil, such as this prism. Some show color zoning from golden brown to a hint of pink.

Topaz tricks
Topaz is sometimes mistaken for diamond. Both are often found in gravel, and they have a similar specific gravity.

Topaz colors
An aluminum silicate of about 20 percent water and fluorine, topaz that has more water is golden brown or pink; with more fluorine it is blue or colorless.

Brazilian Princess
This 21,327-carat topaz was cut in 1977. The largest cut topaz is the 31,000-carat El-Dorado.

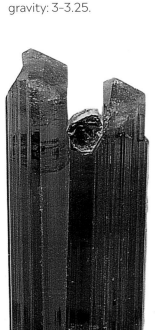

Tourmaline is a brittle mineral.

Tourmaline

This mineral's complex chemistry crystallizes as prisms with flat or wedge-shaped ends. Every crystal has a different structure at each end, giving it an electrical property. If a crystal is warmed, one end becomes positively charged and the other negatively charged.

Tourmaline
comes from the Sinhalese word *turamali,* meaning
"gem pebbles,"
as it is found in gravel beds.

Tourmaline crystal
Crystal system: trigonal; hardness: 7–7.5; specific gravity: 3–3.25.

Tourmaline crystal

Strange attachment
This tourmaline is unusually attached to quartz by a prism face. The pink prism crystallized first, then green tourmaline formed the ends.

Cut stone of two colors of "watermelon" tourmaline

Framed up
This tourmaline prism slice shows threefold symmetry, a triangular cross-section, and the color zones show how it was built up in layers.

Black and green
Tourmaline is pleochroic, which means it is a different color when viewed from different directions.

Set in granite
Gem-quality tourmalines, such as those found in Brazil, are most often in pegmatite veins (p.25) or granites.

Multicolored
Tourmaline shows great color range. Some individual crystals, such as "watermelon," are even more than one color.

Tourmaline crystal

Continued on next page

Continued from previous page

Ring set with almandine garnet

Garnet crystals
Crystal system: cubic; hardness: 6.5–7.5; specific gravity: 3.52–4.32.

Garnet
Garnet is a family of chemically related minerals including almandine, pyrope, spessartine, grossular, and andradite. They can all be found as gemstones; almandine-pyrope is the most widely used. The different chemical compositions mean garnet occurs in most colors other than blue. Sources include South Africa, Brazil, Australia, the US, and Mexico.

Cut demantoid garnet

Demantoid
This emerald-green garnet is the most prized, found in the Ural Mountains, Russia.

Cut pyrope garnet

Pyrope
This deep-red garnet has been mined since the Bronze Age in Bohemia (now Czechia).

Garnet cloisonné
is a style used to **inlay garnet with gold.**

A moustached man stands between two wolves.

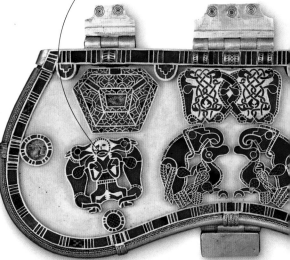

Almandine
Garnet commonly crystallizes as icositetrahedrons, like these almandine crystals. Due to its deep color, almandine is often cut as cabochons (p.59).

Spessartine cabochon

Spessartine
These beautiful orange colors are caused by manganese. Gem-quality crystals are rare.

Fit for a king
This 7th-century purse lid was among many garnet-set pieces found in an Anglo-Saxon royal burial ship in Sutton Hoo, Suffolk, England.

Andradite
Most andradite garnet is not gem quality. Only demantoid, topazolite, and melanite (this black variety) are used as gemstones.

Cut grossular garnets

Color traces
Green grossular contains vanadium; yellow and red contain iron. The red variety is hessonite.

Grossular
Some grossular garnet looks like gooseberries, and the name may come from *grossularia*, which is Latin for gooseberry. This pink grossular from Mexico shows dodecahedral crystals, one of garnet's two main habits.

Peridot

This French word may come from the Arabic *faridat*—"a gem." Peridot is the gem variety of olivine, a magnesium and iron silicate, common in volcanic rocks.

Volcanic bomb
This solidified lava with fragments of olivine-rich rock from deep within Earth was ejected through a volcano.

Peridot crystal
Crystal system: orthorhombic; hardness: 6.5; specific gravity: 3.22–3.40.

Ring set with peridot

Cut peridot from Arizona

Cut peridot from Norway

Cut peridot from Myanmar

Lava

Olivine-rich rock

Island gem
Peridot usually occurs intergrown with other minerals. These crystals with distinct faces (left) came from Zabargad, an Egyptian island in the Red Sea.

Peridot sources

Historically, Egypt was an important source of gem-quality peridot. Now Myanmar (Burma) and, more recently, Pakistan provide large gems, often over 10 carats.

Moonstone

Feldspar is a group of closely-related aluminium silicate minerals of which a few are gems, including moonstone and sunstone. Feldspars are common but rarely gem-quality, ranging in hardness from 6–6.5 and in specific gravity from 2.56–2.76.

Sunstone
The bright spangles in sunstones are reflections from tiny dark-red flakes of hematite.

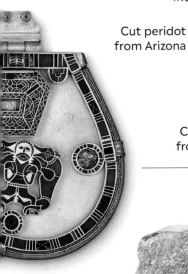

Blue moon
Most moonstones are colorless with a bluish sheen. Some are gray (which may show good cat's-eyes, p.59), orange pink, yellow, or pale green.

Moonstone
This pegmatitic feldspar from Myanmar shows the moonstone sheen. Pegmatites (p.25) may be the source of moonstones from Sri Lankan and Indian gem gravels.

Pin set with sunstone

Ring set with moonstone

Continued on next page

45

Continued from previous page

Spinel

Red and blue spinels can rival ruby and sapphire in color. Until the 19th century, when scientist Romé de l'Isle (p.12) distinguished true ruby from red spinel, red spinels were confusingly called balas rubies. "Balas" may relate to a source in Balascia, now called Badakhshan, in Afghanistan.

Crystal colors
Pure spinel is colorless. The reds and pinks here are due to chromium in the crystals.

Black Prince's Ruby

Lying in state
The Black Prince's Ruby (a 170-carat spinel) is set in the British Imperial State Crown above another famous stone, the Cullinan II diamond (p.35).

The **spinel** called the **Black Prince's Ruby** is set with a small natural **ruby on top**.

Cullinan II diamond

Spinel crystal
Crystal system: cubic; hardness: 8; specific gravity: 3.5–3.7.

Polished over
This crystal has been polished to remove surface blemishes, but still has its octahedral shape.

Small distortion
Spinel usually crystallizes as octahedra, but this crystal aggregate has small distorted octahedra in parallel growth.

Reformed character
This rock from Lake Baikal, Russia, contains octahedra of blue spinel in a matrix of white calcite and muscovite mica. It was probably an impure limestone that recrystallized.

Thorny crystals
These crystallized octahedra from Bodenmais, Germany, are gahnite, a zinc-rich spinel variety. They show spinel's thornlike triangular crystal faces, suggesting its name is from the Latin for thorn—*spina*.

Zircon

Named from the Arabic *zargoon* (golden), zircon comes from localities including Sri Lanka, Thailand, Brazil, South Africa, and Australia. Colorless zircon looks like diamond in luster and fire, but it is softer and may look "sleepy" due to inclusions and double refraction (p.18).

Natural colors
Zircon is zirconium silicate, colorless when pure, but found in a wide range of colors due to different impurities.

Zircon crystal
Crystal system: tetragonal; hardness 7.5; specific gravity: 4.6–4.7.

Radioactive
This large pebble from Sri Lanka is a typical zircon color. Some zircons contain so much uranium and thorium that radioactivity breaks down the crystal structure, making the stone amorphous, or noncrystalline.

Heat treatment
Heating red-brown zircon crystals in an oxygen-free atmosphere produces blue zircon; heating in air (with oxygen) produces golden; colorless can be produced by both methods. These colors may fade, but reheating can restore them.

Natural brown zircon crystals

Heat-treated blue zircon

Stones cut from heat-treated zircon

Chrysoberyl

Only diamond and corundum exceed gem chrysoberyl in hardness. The yellow, green, and brown colors are caused by iron or chromium. There are three varieties: clear yellow-green gems, cat's-eye or cymophane, and alexandrite, famous for its dramatic color change and the best of which come from Russia.

Popular in Portugal
Yellow-green chrysoberyls from Brazil became popular in Portuguese jewellery in the 18th and 19th centuries.

Chrysoberyl crystal
Crystal system: orthorhombic; hardness: 8.5; specific gravity: 3.68–3.78.

Cut alexandrite in natural light

Cut alexandrite in artificial light

Russian alexandrite
Discovered in 1830 in the Ural Mountains on Tsar Alexander II's birthday (hence the name), alexandrite looks green by day and red in artificial light—Russia's imperial colors.

Cut yellow chrysoberyl

Collectors' items

There are more than 4,000 mineral species, but crucial factors such as hardness (pp.18–19), durability, and rarity reduce the number of commercial gems to about 100. Many people collect rare gems of exceptional size or color, or cut minerals that are too soft or fragile for jewelry, such as blende and sphene. Benitoite, on the other hand, is durable but rare.

Tanzanite
This gem variety of zoisite, found in 1967 in Tanzania, is rare for its blue, violet, and yellow-gray displays. Many greenish gray crystals are heat-treated to be blue.

Danburite
This mineral was first found as colorless crystals in a pegmatite (p.25) in Danbury, Connecticut (hence its name). More colorless stones come from countries such as Japan, Mexico, Russia, Madagascar, and Bolivia.

Sphene
Ranging from yellow-brown to emerald-green, sphene has great luster and fire but is soft. The finest gems come from the US, the Swiss Alps, and Myanmar (Burma).

Cordierite
Showing very strong pleochroism, from blue to yellowish gray, this gem was used by the Vikings to navigate their longboats (p.60) and led to them being called "water sapphires." Gem-quality cordierite comes from Sri Lanka, Myanmar, Madagascar, and India.

Alpine experts
Many fine Alpine crystals are collected by strahlers—experienced mountaineers who are talented mineral collectors.

Axinite

Beautiful wedge-shaped crystals of brown axinite from Bourg d'Oisans, France, display gray and violet flashes in different directions. Once very rare, more crystals are being found in Sri Lanka, Norway, South America, the US, and Tanzania.

Blende

Sphalerite, or blende, is the world's major source of zinc. It is normally opaque gray to black, but gem-quality yellow, green, and reddish brown crystals come from Mexico and Spain. However, they are too soft for jewelry.

Benitoite

These crystals from San Benito County, California, are comparable in color to fine sapphires and display similar fire to diamonds, but are very rare.

Blende crystals in matrix

Rough blende crystal

Cut fibrolite

Cut andalusite

The San Benito Mine in 1914 showing the open cut and an ore bucket on the left

Fibrolite

This 19.84-carat rare variety of the mineral sillimanite is from Myanmar. It is one of the world's biggest. Andalusite is also made of aluminum silicate but has a different structure—gem-quality stones from Brazil and Sri Lanka show pleochroic red and green.

Scapolite

These gems occur in pastel shades of pink, yellow, and purple, and as fine cat's-eyes (p.59).

Cut kunzite

Spodumene

Magnificent spodumene crystals come from Brazil, California, and Afghanistan. Fine gems are cut from pale-green, yellow, and pink crystals—the latter, kunzite, is named after G.F. Kunz, a US mineralogist. Rare, green hiddenite is found in North Carolina and Sri Lanka.

Sinhalite

Thought to be Sri Lankan peridot, sinhalite was proven in 1950 to be a new species and named after an old name for Sri Lanka—Sinhala.

Kunzite crystal

Cut pale-green spodumene

Malachite

This vivid green copper mineral is 4 on the hardness scale (pp.18–19) and has a specific gravity of 3.8. Democratic Republic of the Congo, Zambia, Namibia, Australia, and Russia are the main sources.

Lapis lazuli

This is not a single mineral but a rock of blue lazurite with variable amounts of calcite and pyrite. The best, from Afghanistan, is mostly lazurite, a deep blue, and 5.5 in hardness with a specific gravity of 2.7–2.9. Other sources exist in Russia and Chile.

Stones for carving

Microcrystalline rocks and minerals have been used as decoration for thousands of years. Ancient civilizations such as the Egyptians, Chinese, and Sumerians used jade, turquoise, and lapis for jewelry and carvings.

Turquoise tradition
Most turquoise is produced in the southwestern US, and traditional Indigenous American jewelry is still made here.

Turquoise

Turquoise occurs in nodules and veins of green or blue: copper makes it blue, while iron makes it green. It has a specific gravity of 2.6–2.9 and a hardness of 5–6.

White calcite

Persian blue
The name lapis lazuli is derived from the Persian word for blue. Its color is caused by sulfur.

Natural mosaic
Turquoise most often occurs in mosaics. The finest blue turquoise comes from Iran (previously Persia).

Popular jewel
Lapis lazuli has been used for beads and other jewelry.

Blue Persian turquoise inlaid with gold

Mask of Tezcatlipoca
This 15th–16th century Aztec mask of turquoise and lignum, shaped around a human skull, represents the Aztec god Tezcatlipoca.

Medieval painting
Lapis lazuli was crushed and purified in medieval times to make the paint pigment ultramarine, used in the Wilton Diptych altarpiece (above).

Jade

The Spanish conquerors of Mexico believed the Indigenous Americans' green stones would cure kidney ailments. They called them kidney stones, or *piedra de hyada*, and from this the word jade was derived. In 1863, they were proved to be two different minerals, now called jadeite and nephrite.

Life jacket
The ancient Chinese believed jade could give life and so placed plates of nephrite around a corpse to try to preserve it. This is a 2nd-century-BCE funeral suit of a princess.

Jadeite
Mainly found in Myanmar (Burma), jadeite varies widely in color. The most prized is the emerald-green jadeite known as imperial jade. Jadeite has a hardness of 6.5–7 and a specific gravity of 3.3–3.5.

Jadeite fashioned into a ball

Nephrite design by Russian jeweler Fabergé

Chinese camel
This nephrite camel was carved in China. White and cream nephrites contain very little iron. More iron causes green and black stones.

Nephrite
Used by the Māoris of New Zealand, it has a hardness of 6.5 and specific gravity of 2.9–3.1.

Other stones
Many other stones are popular for carving, mainly because of their color. These include malachite, Blue John, serpentine, and rhodonite.

Serpentine
Carvers can use the snakeskin patterns in serpentine for works of art. Some is soft and easy to carve, but the yellow-green bowenite, favored by Chinese carvers, is up to 6 in hardness.

Bowenite, a hard, compact variety of serpentine

Rhodonite
Rhodo means pink; its color is caused by manganese. It has a hardness of about 6 and is used for carving and inlays.

Blue John
This purple and pale yellow, banded fluorite comes from Derbyshire, England. It is fragile, so is usually bonded with resins to make it more hard-wearing.

19th-century Blue John vase

Precious metals

Gold, silver, and platinum are crystalline, although single crystals are rare. Gold and silver were among the earliest metals worked, but today platinum is also valuable. All three are relatively soft, easy to work, and hard to destroy, and have high SGs (p.18).

Latrobe nugget
This crystalline gold nugget was found in 1855 in the presence of His Excellency C.J. Latrobe, Governor of the colony of Victoria, Australia.

Gold

Gold is used for measuring wealth. Pure gold (24 carats) is a dense (SG = 19.3) but soft (H = 2.5–3) metal. Before it can be used, it has to be refined, and it is often alloyed with other metals to make it harder.

Worth its weight
The golden Buddha of Bangkok is 6 tons (5.5 metric tons) of gold, worth more than $250 million (£215 million).

The statue is present in the temple of Wat Traimit, Bangkok, Thailand.

This trophy head was attached to the ceremonial sword belonging to the king of Asante.

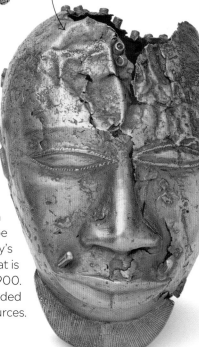

Gold sandwich
Gold is sometimes found in hydrothermal veins, associated with quartz, as in this quartz vein from New Zealand.

Rare sight
Gold usually occurs as fine grains scattered through a rock, or as "invisible gold," making this group of crystals from Zimbabwe very rare.

Built on gold
The Asante kingdom (producers of this trophy head—an ornament in the shape of a defeated enemy's face) dominated what is now Ghana in 1700–1900. Its power was founded upon its gold resources.

Platinum

Platinum is used in modern technology, as a standard weight, for surgical instruments, and in jewelry. Its name means little silver. Platinum is often found in granules or small nuggets in placer deposits in Russia, Canada, and South Africa.

Platinum crown
The Crown of Queen Elizabeth The Queen Mother is made of platinum.

Big nugget
This 2.4-lb (1.1-kg) nugget of platinum from the Ural Mountains, Russia, is unusually large.

Rich layer
This platinum-bearing pyroxenite comes from igneous rock in South Africa called the Merensky Reef. It is only 12 in (30 cm) thick but is rich in platinum.

Rounded
Platinum is quite soft (H = 4–4.5); it is unusual to find sharp crystals.

Silver

Silver crystals are rare, but cubic crystals have been found. Silver usually occurs as massive minerals or as thick, wiry aggregates. It has a hardness of 2.5–3. In medieval times, silver was more valuable than gold. Today, metallic silver is used in electronics and photography.

In need of a polish
This dendritic growth (p.23) of silver crystals from Chile is slightly tarnished.

Silver wire
These wiry silver crystals, with quartz and calcite, are from the once-famous silver locality of Kongsberg, Norway.

Bonus
Silver is now mostly a by-product from copper and lead-zinc mining. These galena (a lead sulphide) crystals come from Eire, Republic of Ireland.

Organic
gems

Gems from animals and plants, such as amber, jet, coral, pearl, and shell, are called organic. They are not as hard (4 or less) or as dense (1.04—amber to 2.78—pearl) as gemstones, but are popular due to their beauty. Pearls have long been greatly valued, while shell and amber have been found in ancient graves from 2000 BCE.

Jet and amber

Jet and amber both come from trees. Jet is a fine-grained, black rock formed over millions of years from rotted and compressed trees. Amber is the fossilized resin, or sap, of trees.

Ancient traveler

The south and east coasts of the Baltic Sea are major sources of amber, which is slightly denser than seawater and can be carried across the sea.

Jet black

This jet contains fossils of several long-extinct animals, including an ammonite. Jet is hard-wearing and can be polished.

Fossil ammonite of marine origin

Coral

Reef-builing coral is a skeleton of calcium carbonate made by colonies of animals in warm waters. The range of colors is due to different growth conditions and organic contents.

Distinctive pitted surface

Necklace material

From the species *Heliopora caerules*, this blue coral grows around the Philippines, Australia, and Japan. It is often cut into beads.

Coral living in a warm sea

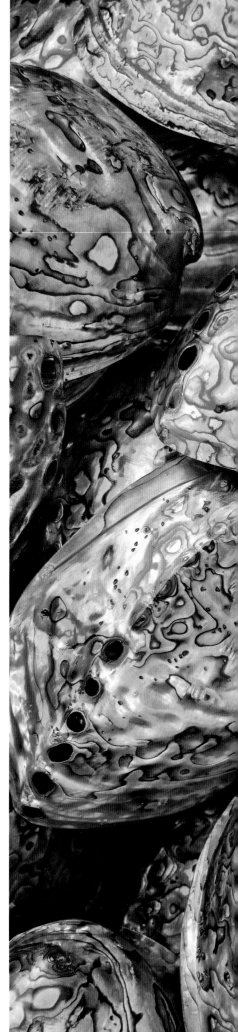

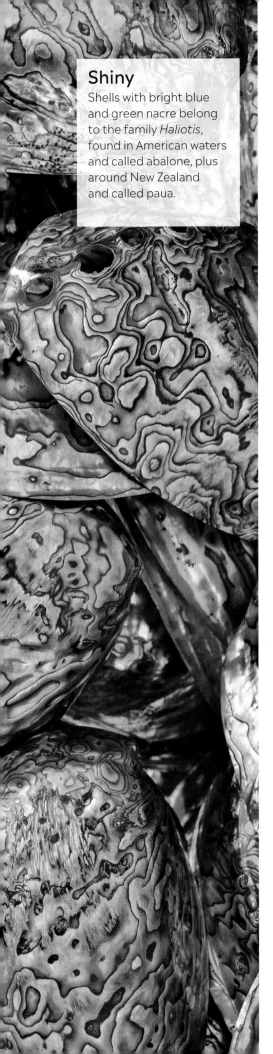

Shiny

Shells with bright blue and green nacre belong to the family *Haliotis*, found in American waters and called abalone, plus around New Zealand and called paua.

Pearl and shell

The sheen on pearls and some shells is caused by light reflecting on platelets of calcium carbonate called nacre. Pearls form in shells when an irritant such as sand gets stuck in the shell and the animal surrounds it with nacre.

Oyster catchers

For more than 2,000 years, the Arabian Gulf has supplied pearls, recovered by divers. Today, an irritant is put into oysters and shells are farmed for pearls.

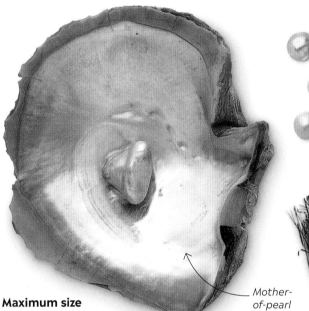

Pearls of color

Pearls' many colors include yellow, pink, and cream.

Mother-of-pearl

Maximum size

The best pearls come from oysters and mussels. *Pinctada maxima* is the largest pearl oyster.

Mumbai bunch

In Mumbai (formerly Bombay), India, different pearl sizes were strung on silk, then combined with strings of other sizes suitable for a necklace.

Indian ruby

Canning jewel

Irregularly shaped pearls are called baroque pearls. Four, including one forming the body, are in the Canning Triton jewel, probably made in the late 16th century in south Germany.

Tassels made of silver wire

55

What price?

Gem values can vary, even within one species. This 57.26-carat sapphire is of such size and fine color that it can only be valued if it is sold.

What is it worth?

The market value of gems plays a large part in persuading people to buy them. Stones have been cut to enhance their beauty, and traded so people can display their style or wealth. Ruby, pearl, emerald, diamond, and sapphire have been popular since medieval times.

Jean Baptiste Tavernier

This Frenchman traveled Europe and Asia in the 17th century, trading gems. His detailed journals are used to research famous diamonds.

Not cheap

Growing synthetic crystals (pp.26–27) is expensive. Stones cut from them are therefore not cheap, but natural stones still cost many times more.

Cut synthetic ruby

Short-lasting

Red glass is used to imitate ruby, but its luster fades. Ruby's hardness and toughness keeps its qualities for longer.

Synthetic ruby crystals

This synthetic ruby boule was made using Auguste Verneuil's flame fusion method.

Priceless

Painite is priceless and very few crystals have been found. It was discovered in Myanmar (Burma) by gem dealer A.C.D. Pain and was named after him.

Weight in beans

Carob tree seeds have long been used as a standard for comparing gem weight. In the 20th century, a standard weight similar to the carob seed's—the carat—was agreed internationally with a standard of 0.007 oz (0.2 g).

The term carat comes from the Greek word for carob seeds—*keration*.

Carob pod

Carob seed

1-carat ruby

Strontium titanate

Synthetic rutile

Fluorite

Quartz

Fake diamonds

In the 1800s, Faulkner's Celebrated Diamonds were touted as "The only perfect substitute for diamonds of first water."

Lithium niobate

Stone substitutes

Diamond is the most frequently imitated stone in jewellery. The oldest imitations are glass and rock crystal, but in the 20th century synthetic versions became available. These diamond simulants are arranged clockwise, from fluorite, in order of increasing fire.

Topaz

Cubic zirconia

Synthetic sapphire

Details of proportions, clarity, and color are listed

Zircon

Diamond

YAG (yttrium aluminum garnet)

GGG (gadolinium gallium garnet)

Glass

Synthetic spinel

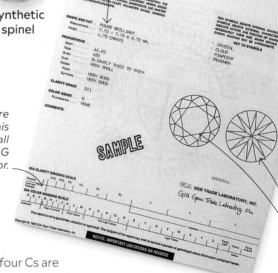
GIA GEM TRADE LABORATORY, INC.

DIAMOND GRADING REPORT

SAMPLE

Clarity and color are graded on a scale. This diamond is graded SI₁ (small inclusion) for clarity and G (near colorless) for color.

Chipped glass of a GTD

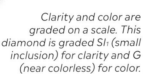

Doubled up

A stone made of two materials fused together is known as a doublet. In the popular garnet-topped doublet (GTD), the top is a thin piece of garnet, which is more durable than the color-providing glass base. These cheaper stones are sometimes sold by disreputable traders as rubies, sapphires, or emeralds.

Four Cs

Two diamonds that look alike can have different values. The four Cs are characteristics that determine value: cut, weight in carats, color, and clarity. In 1975, a standardized grading procedure was adopted by many countries for consistency.

The positions of any inclusions are indicated on the outlines of the crown and pavilion.

Slocum stone

Made to match

True opal is graded according to body color and the play of colors. Black opal is rare and the most expensive. Opal is imitated in several ways. Slocum stone is glass and much cheaper; Gilson opal is grown in the laboratory and is intermediate in value.

Polystyrene latex

Real black opal

Gilson opal

Cutting gems

Some crystals are beautiful in shape, luster, and color, but most are imperfect. A lapidary (skilled polisher and stone cutter) can turn them into valuable objects of beauty. Beads and cabochons are old cuts, such as for turquoise (p.50). Today, brilliant-cut diamonds are the most popular form.

Brilliant-cut rutile
In 1919, Marcel Tolkowsky set the specifications of a brilliant cut to give the best sparkle, brilliance, and fire.

Rose-cut smoky quartz
Dating from the 14th century, the rose cut has a flat base and a dome-shaped top covered in triangular facets.

Table-cut amethyst
Derived from the diamond octahedron by sawing off the top.

Step-cut emerald
This cut has many rectangular facets, suitable for strongly colored gems.

Cutting a brilliant
A lapidary first studies a rough stone with a loupe (powerful lens) to find any flaws. The stone is marked to show where it should be sawed and the facets are ground.

Brilliant recut
The Koh-i-noor diamond (p.35) was recut into a brilliant in 1852. Here, the Duke of Wellington makes the first facet, with Amsterdam cutter Mr. Voorsanger.

Koh-i-noor brilliant cut

1 **Choice**
A rough crystal is chosen.

Crown

Bezel

Girdle

2 **Sawed in two**
The crystal is sawed to remove the top pyramid and rounded by grinding against another diamond, called bruting.

Pavilion

Table facet

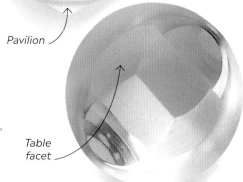

3 **Faceting begins**
The stone is mounted on a dop (stick) and the flat table facet is ground on a scaife (cast-iron wheel).

4 **Further facets**
Three sets of four bezel facets are ground: between the table and girdle, on the pavilion, on the crown, plus a culet facet on the base.

5 **Finished off**
A brillianteer adds 24 facets above and 16 below the girdle. A standard brilliant has 57 facets (58 with a culet).

Diamond cutter's table in the 19th century

Triangular-cut citrine

Irregular-cut sapphire

Cutting it fine

Diamond-cutting tools of the 15th century were only replaced with the development of automatic machines and lasers in the 20th century.

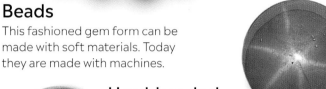

Agate

Amethyst

Beads

This fashioned gem form can be made with soft materials. Today they are made with machines.

Hard-headed

Hard-wearing opaque materials, such as this garnet, are often cut as cabochons—rounds or ovals with plain, curved surfaces.

Light display

Star sapphires and rubies (p.37) are cut as cabochons for the rutile to reflect the light and show the star.

Quartz cabochons in a brooch, cut to display the cat's-eye effect

Special cuts

A special cut may be developed for a rare stone, to keep its weight, or for special occasions.

Heart-cut heliodor

Groove caused by polishing garnet cabochons

Over and over

Tumbling rocks and minerals in a drum with water and grit (coarse grit to start, fine grit to finish) polishes them.

Indian polish

This large corundum was used in India in the 19th century for fashioning and polishing garnets. Over time, tiny chips split off, eventually leaving grooves.

Grinding

Stones are held against a grinding wheel to give them a rough shape. Gem cutters use wax to hold the gem in place on a dop stick.

Lore and legend

Superstition and myth have long been attached to crystals. In Persian mythology, the world is said to stand on a giant sapphire, coloring the skies blue. Emeralds were once thought to blind snakes, diamonds were thought to be medicinal, and rubies were symbols of power in the Middle Ages. Some crystals are said to be cursed, bringing disaster to their owners.

Crystal compass

The Vikings may have navigated with transparent cordierite crystals. When held up to sunlight and rotated, cordierite darkens and changes color, which could be used to figure out compass directions.

Migrating birds

A magnetic crystal in birds' brains may detect Earth's magnetic field.

Power to repel

Some pieces of magnetite (an iron oxide) are magnetic. Known as lodestones, they were once believed to have special powers; Alexander the Great gave lodestones to his soldiers to repel evil spirits.

Iron filings attracted to magnetite follow magnetic lines of force

Magnetite crystals

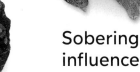

Stone tears

Staurolite crystals can twin at right angles to form crosses, and were used as amulets at baptisms. Those in Patrick County, Virginia, are called fairy stones, from the legend that they crystallized from the sad tears of fairies upon Christ's death.

Sobering influence

In the 15th century, amethyst was believed to cure drunkenness. This may be because drinking vessels were sometimes made of amethyst, and made water look like red wine, and so had no intoxicating effect!

Holy rows

The original breastplate of the High Priest of Israel is described in the Bible (Exodus 28,15–30) as set with four rows of three stones. The stones are all named, but some are misleading. The sapphire, for example, is actually lapis lazuli.

Crystal gazing

Crystal balls have been used for telling the future for thousands of years. The fortune teller gazes at the polished surface until they can no longer focus on the ball but see instead a curtain of mist, enabling "visions" to be seen, imagined for the person whose fortune is being told.

Visionary
John Dee was an advisor to England's Queen Elizabeth I. He conducted crystal gazings for her, but many thought he was a fraud.

For the future
Quartz is the most popular material for crystal balls, but other materials with a shiny surface have been known to be used.

Birthstones

A special stone dedicated to each month of the year was first suggested in the 1st century CE, linked to the 12 stones in the High Priest's breastplate. Wearing such stones became popular in the 18th century, first in Poland.

Changes
The gem for each month varied over time, with different Roman, Arabian, Jewish, and Russian combinations. The group here is popular today.

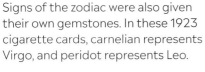

On the cards
Signs of the zodiac were also given their own gemstones. In these 1923 cigarette cards, carnelian represents Virgo, and peridot represents Leo.

December (Turquoise)

January (Garnet)

November (Topaz)

February (Amethyst)

October (Opal)

March (Aquamarine)

Rock crystal engraved with the 12 signs of the zodiac

April (Diamond)

September (Sapphire)

July (Ruby)

June (Pearl)

May (Emerald)

August (Peridot)

Some **Hindus** believe keeping a **ruby** ensures good health and wealth.

At home

Many items at home are crystalline, including ice crystals in the freezer, salt crystals in food, and silicon crystal chips in the fridge and washing machine. The TV and camera work due to crystals, the house is built of crystalline materials, and cars stand outside, slowly rusting—crystallizing!

Greatly enlarged photograph of crystals of vitamin C

Spoonful of sugar

More than 100 million tons of sugar are crystallized every year in refineries, from the liquid solution of raw sugar cane or beet. Even this spoon is a mass of silver crystals.

Liquid crystals were known since **1888, but**

in 1963, US scientist **George Heilmier** suggested using them as LCDs.

Vital intake

These tablets have crystals of ascorbic acid, or vitamin C, in them—a white crystalline substance in plants, especially citrus fruits, tomatoes, and green vegetables. Vitamins are essential for health but cannot be produced by the body, and so are taken in through food or tablets.

Liquid crystal display

Liquid crystal display (LCD)

Liquid crystals are not truly crystalline. They flow like liquid but have properties, and molecules arranged, like crystals. Power rearranges molecules to reflect or absorb light.

Jagadish Chandra Bose
Indian scientist Jagadish Chandra Bose (1858–1937) researched how to use crystals to detect electromagnetic waves. In 1901, he patented a microwave detector made of galena crystals.

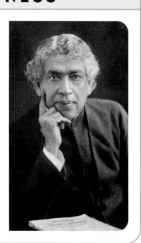

Pressed for time

Quartz crystals keep time (p.31), and synthetic rubies (pp.26–27) are used for watch bearings.

Kettle fur

Harmless minerals in tap water crystallize and coat the inside of a tea kettle when the water is boiled.

Needlelike crystals in kettle fur

Precious stones

Many people own jewelry with precious stones. This silver brooch contains diamonds, a blue sapphire, and a pearl.

Amethyst crystals

Cat litter

Cat litter is primarily made of clay and other minerals that absorb moisture and bad smells. Crystallized silica added to the litter gives it a "clumping" quality.

Cavity fillers
Fluids in basaltic lava flows often percolate through rocks and crystallize in available cavities.

Hand lens for studying crystal features

Collecting

Crystals can be collected in the field, bought, or exchanged with friends and dealers. They are usually fragile and should be carefully stored with details of where they were found and, if possible, their host rock.

In miniature
Tiny micromount specimens allow fine crystal groups of rare and unusual minerals to be easily stored by collectors.

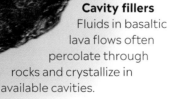

Wulfenite crystal

Did you **know?**

FASCINATING FACTS

The Persians thought Earth sat on a giant sapphire and the blue skies were its reflection. Others thought the sky was a sapphire, in which Earth was set.

Sapphire-blue is a color associated with harmony, trust, and loyalty, which is why many women have sapphires in their engagement rings.

The name garnet comes from the Latin for pomegranate, a fruit with bright red, garnetlike seeds. Red garnet colors vary from violet-red to burgundy.

Diamonds can be found under the sea. People trawl for them in large, offshore ships, which pump gravel containing diamonds up to the surface.

Diamonds in kimberlite rock are mined on a huge scale. More than 27.5 tons (25 metric tons) of rock are blasted for every finished carat— 0.007 oz (0.2 g)— of diamond mined.

In medieval times, rich people wore diamonds to protect them from the plague. The ancient Greeks thought diamonds protected against poisons.

Sapphire and diamond pendant

Moonstones are often set in silver, to bring out their silvery sheen.

Moonstone necklace

People used to think a moonstone's opalescent luster waxed and waned like the Moon, so moonstones were worn by Moon worshippers.

Topaz crystals can be more than 3.25 ft (1 meter) long and weigh several hundred kilos. "Topaz" is thought to come from the Sanskrit word for *tapas*, meaning "fire."

The ancient Greeks believed amber was the hardened rays of a sunset and sacred to the sun god Apollo. Amber can produce an electric charge when rubbed; "electricity" comes from the Greek word for amber, *elektron*.

Pomegranate

Hawksbill turtle

Tortoiseshell carapace was widely used for hair ornaments.

Tortoiseshell actually comes from turtles, from the shell of the rare (now protected) Hawksbill turtle. Most "tortoiseshell" in jewelry today is made of plastic.

Six-rayed star sapphires were once thought to protect against evil. The star's three crossing arms were meant to represent faith, hope, and destiny.

The ancient Egyptians believed lapis lazuli's intense blue made it heavenly, using it on statues of their gods and in burial masks to protect them in the next life.

Star sapphire

Cultivating pearls (making them grow by putting irritants into oysters) is faster than waiting for natural pearls to form, but it can still take more than a year.

Diamond dredging boats

QUESTIONS AND ANSWERS

How long have people been mining for gemstones?

Jewelry containing gems has been found in burial sites dating back thousands of years. Some ancient Egyptian pieces, made of gold and set with gems, have also survived.

What are potato stones?

Also known as thunder eggs, potato stones are geodes—hollow balls of rock with crystals inside. The crystals form when silica-rich liquids seep into bubbles of cooling lava.

Potato stones

Why are gemstones so precious?

Because of their natural beauty, durability, rarity, and how they are cut and polished. There are 4,000 kinds of minerals, but only about 100 are gemstones, making them rare.

Where do diamonds come from?

Diamonds form at high pressure and temperatures deep inside Earth. Diamonds were first found 2,000 years ago in river gravel. Today, most diamonds are mined from kimberlite rock. Some of the main producers include Russia, Botswana, and Canada.

What are seed pearls?

Pearls vary in size. The smallest are seed pearls. Pearls are not weighed in carats, but in grains. One grain = 0.002 oz (0.05 g). Seed pearls weigh less than 0.25 of a grain.

Why were children often given coral jewelry in the past?

To keep them healthy and safe; coral was thought to protect from evil.

Scarab beetle good-luck charm, found in Tutankhamun's tomb

Why are emeralds green?

The green of emeralds comes from chromium and vanadium.

Why are gemstones cut and polished?

Cutting and polishing maximizes the amount of light they reflect so that they sparkle and shine.

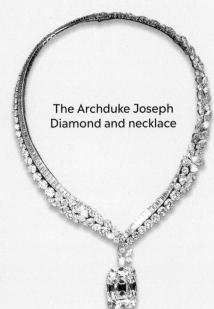

The Archduke Joseph Diamond and necklace

Why are organic gems often carved rather than cut into facets?

Organic gems, such as coral and pearl, are soft and often opaque, so light cannot shine through them, making it pointless to cut them into facets to increase their brilliance.

What is the connection between rubies and emery boards?

Ruby is a variety of the mineral corundum, which is second in hardness to diamond. Emery is an impure form of corundum, and has been used as an abrasive for thousands of years.

Which famous ruby isn't really a ruby at all?

Many crown jewels around the world contain red gemstones called spinels, which people mistook for rubies. The huge Black Prince's Ruby in the British Imperial State Crown is in fact a spinel.

Cut ruby

RECORD BREAKERS

MOST VALUABLE GEMSTONE:
Diamonds, Earth's hardest mineral, are the most precious, famed for their fiery beauty.

BIGGEST DIAMOND:
The largest rough diamond ever mined was the Cullinan Diamond, found in 1905 in South Africa, weighing 3,106 carats. It was cut into nine large and 96 smaller stones.

CUTTING MARATHON:
It took three polishers eight months to cut and polish the Cullinan 1 Diamond, now set in the British Imperial Sceptre.

LARGEST RUBY:
The "King Ruby" in India is the largest ruby, weighing 48 lb, 6.43 oz (21,955 g).

BIGGEST BERYL CRYSTAL:
A beryl crystal found in Madagascar was 39.6 tons (36 metric tons) and was about 60 ft (18 m) long.

Identifying gemstones

To the untutored eye, many gemstones look alike. They can be similar in color and cut. Here is a guide to the color and characteristics of some of the most popular gemstones.

Emerald lizard

Mixed-cut citrine with the orange tinge often seen in this gem

Citrine
Citrine is a yellow or golden form of quartz. Natural citrine (its name comes from the word "citrus") is pale yellow, but it is extremely rare.

Oval mixed-cut amethyst with a typical purplish-violet color

Amethyst
Amethysts are purple quartz crystals, often with distinctive internal markings and a blue or reddish tinge.

Tiger's-eye, cut and polished to show off its stripes

Tiger's-eye
This chalcedony variety is a quartz-type made up of tiny fibers. It looks waxy and is black with yellow and brown stripes.

Carnelian
Also called cornelian, this is a translucent, reddish-orange or brown form of chalcedony.

Typical reddish-orange polished stone from India

Colorless, brilliant-cut diamond with black inclusions

Diamond
Made of pure carbon, diamond is very hard and shines brightly. The most popular variety is pure and colorless.

Bright red cushion mixed-cut ruby

Ruby
The expensive, classic ruby is a rich red, but color varies from pink to brown. Rubies are hard, second to diamonds.

Pale blue Sri Lankan sapphire

Sapphire
The most valuable are a clear, deep blue, but can be yellow, green, pink, or colorless. It is a type of corundum.

Bluish-green emerald with many tiny fissures and internal markings

Emerald
This beryl variety is a rich green. The finest are transparent and flawless. Most have flaws called a *jardin* (garden).

Octagonal step-cut aquamarine with a slight greenish tinge

Aquamarine
This beryl variety ranges from pale sea-green to dark blue. It can seem to change color from different angles.

An opal displaying flashes of green and blue

Opal
Known for its iridescence and flashes of color. Iridescent opal with a dark background is black opal. "Potch opal" is opaque, without any iridescence.

Salmon-pink colored topaz

Topaz
Topaz occurs in several different colors, ranging from deep golden yellow (known as sherry topaz) and pink to blue and green. Natural pink stones are extremely rare.

Tourmaline
Tourmalines come in a range of colors, but they all have the same crystal structure.

Watermelon tourmaline

Garnet

The most popular types of garnets for jewelry are pyrope, which is blood-red, and the deep red almandine.

Pyrope (garnet) cut as an oval

Octagonal mixed-cut peridot

Peridot

This olive or bottle-green colored gem has a waxy luster and strong double refraction.

A gray moonstone

Moonstone

Some are gray, yellow, pink, or green. The name comes from its blue-white sheen.

Octagonal mixed-cut with a vitreous luster

Spinel

The most popular is ruby-red, but it can also be blue and yellow. Red spinels were once known as balas rubies.

Cut yellow chrysoberyl

Chrysoberyl

This gem is known for its golden color. One variety, alexandrite, appears to change from green to light red in artificial light.

Colorless zircon produced by heating a reddish-brown stone

Zircon

Pure zircon is colorless and resembles diamond, but it is more likely to be golden brown.

Translucent jadeite with black inclusions

Jade

Two different minerals, jadeite and nephrite, are known as jade. The finest jadeite is emerald green. Nephrite varies from cream to olive green.

Polished rock speckled with pyrite

Lapis lazuli

Prized for its intense dark blue, lapis lazuli is a rock made up of several minerals. Specks or streaks of pale pyrite and calcite are often visible.

Stone cut and polished as a cabochon

Turquoise

Turquoise is valued for its color, which varies from blue–green to bright blue. Opaque, it is usually cut and polished into rounded beads or cabochons.

ORGANIC GEMSTONES

Organic gems are derived from plants and animals. Amber, jet, coral, pearl, ivory, and shell are all organics. These materials are not stones and they are not as hard and durable as mineral gems. Instead of being cut into facets, they are usually polished or carved.

Carved jet with a rose at the center

JET

This fine-grained rock formed from fossilized wood. Black or very dark brown, it is opaque with a velvety luster. It is sometimes faceted and polished.

AMBER

Amber forms from the hardened resin of trees. Transparent or translucent, it is usually a golden orange, but can also be a dark red. It sometimes contains insects and plants.

Amber necklace

Transparent golden brown beads that have been faceted

CORAL

Made of the remains of coral polyps, it can be pink, red, white, or blue.

Intricate red coral carving showing a monkey climbing a tree

PEARL

Formed in shellfish, with an iridescent sheen, they vary from white and cream with a hint of pink to brown, or black.

A roughly spherical pearl suitable to be used as a bead

Find out more

Natural history and geological museums usually have extensive rock and mineral displays, and are an invaluable source of information on how crystals formed and what they look like in their natural state. Many also have good gemstone collections. There are many places where you can see how precious gems have been used in jewelry. Here are some suggestions for visiting and websites for browsing.

Crystals and gemstones

In most natural history and geological collections—such as the ones found at the Natural History Museum in London—are displays of cut gemstones and famous jewels. There are also crystals and gemstones in their natural state, often still embedded in their matrix (host) rock.

KEY TO SYMBOLS

Diamond	Ruby	Sapphire	Emerald
Aquamarine	Chrysoberyl	Topaz	Tourmaline
Peridot	Garnet	Pearl	Opal

Where gems are found

Where gemstones are found depends on the geological conditions. This map shows the main locations of 12 of the most popular and highly prized gems. If you visit any of these areas, you may be able to visit mines or see samples of the gemstones in local galleries, museums, and shops.

Gem collections

Why not start a gem collection of your own? Look for specimens on beaches, riverbanks, and hillsides. Clean your finds with water and arrange them in small cardboard trays. Try taking them to your local museum for help in identifying them.

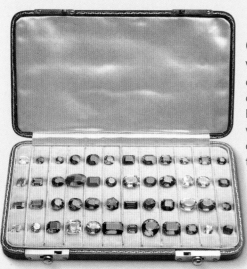

Cut gemstones that form part of the Matthews Collection in London

USEFUL WEBSITES

- Learn about crystals and gems and find lots of resources and fun activities: **www.smithsonianeducation.org**
- See pictures of more than 1,000 different types of minerals: **www.webmineral.com**
- View the Smithsonian Gem and Mineral Collection: **www.gimizu.de/sgmcol**
- Find facts on more than 60 popular colored gemstones: **www.gemstone.org**

Jewels and jewelry

A museum of decorative arts will show you how gems have been set in jewelry over the ages, from historic pieces to modern jewelry in different styles. Try visiting a museum's ancient Egyptian section for early jewelry. If you travel abroad, visit local craft museums to see samples of local traditional jewelry.

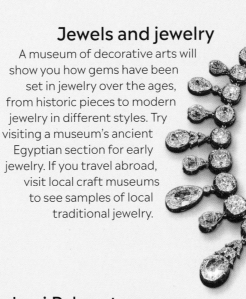

Napoleon I diamond necklace from the Smithsonian Institution, Washington, D.C.

Topkapi Palace treasury

If you go to Istanbul in Turkey, visit the Topkapi Palace Museum, which has a collection of Colombian emeralds set in jewelry and other accessories. As well as this dagger, there is a golden throne studded with tourmaline, a carved emerald snuffbox, and vases carved from exquisite green jadeite.

Dagger with emeralds set into the hilt

Charlemagne (742–814), king of the Franks

Gold set with precious jewels

Crown of Empress Eugénie on display at the Louvre, Paris, France

Golden sceptre set with gemstones, made for Charles V in 1380

Crown Jewels

Examples of famous gems set in gold and silver are on display in the Crown Jewels of France, Britain, and Austria. At the Louvre in Paris are the coronation crowns of Napoleon and Louis XV, plus scepters, swords, and the Regent—one of the world's purest diamonds, worn by Louis XV at his coronation in 1722. The British Crown Jewels at the Tower of London include many jewels still used in state ceremonies today, such as the Imperial State Crown with the famous Black Prince's Ruby.

The Tower of London Education Center in London, where schoolchildren can try on replicas of the Crown Jewels and royal cloaks, as well as armor

Glossary

ALLOCHROMATIC Meaning "other-colored," it describes colorless gems that are colored by impurities.

ALLUVIAL DEPOSITS Weathered rock fragments that have been carried along in rivers and streams and deposited.

AMORPHOUS Without a regular internal atomic structure or external shape.

ASTERISM The star effect seen in some gems, such as rubies and sapphires, when they are cut into cabochons.

BIREFRINGENCE (DR) Double refraction, a crystal property in which light passing through is split into two rays.

Brilliant-cut diamond

BRILLIANT CUT The most popular cut for diamonds and many other stones. The standard brilliant has 57 facets, or 58 if the gem is cut with a flat face at the base.

CABOCHON A type of cut in which a gemstone is cut into a round or oval with a plain, domed upper surface.

Star ruby cut into a cabochon

CARAT The standard measure of weight for gemstones. One carat equals 0.007 oz (0.2 g).

CHATOYANCY The tiger's-eye effect of some stones when cut into cabochons.

CLEAVAGE The way in which a crystal splits apart along certain well-defined planes according to its internal structure.

COMPOSITION The fixed or well-defined chemical makeup of a mineral.

COMPOUND Two or more elements joined together chemically, which can only be separated by heat or great pressure.

CORE The area of iron and nickel at the center of Earth.

CRUST The thin outermost layer of Earth.

CRYSTAL A naturally occurring solid with a regular internal structure and smooth faces.

CRYSTALLINE Having a crystal structure.

CUT The way a gem is cut into a number of flat faces called facets, or rounded and polished.

DENDRITES Fernlike growths of crystals that line rock cracks and joints.

Dendrites of the mineral pyrolusite

DICHROIC A term that is used to describe a gem that appears to be two different colors when viewed from different directions.

DIFFRACTION The splitting of white light into its constituent colors.

DOUBLET A composite stone made of two pieces cemented or glued together.

DURABILITY The capacity to last for a long time without wearing out.

EROSION The wearing away of land and rocks by a moving medium, such as water or ice.

FACET One flat surface of a cut gemstone.

FACETING Cutting and polishing gems into flat surfaces.

FIRE A term used for dispersed

light. A gem with strong fire sparkles with the colors of the rainbow.

FLUORESCENCE Colored light that radiates from a mineral when it is exposed to invisible ultraviolet light.

GEMSTONE Mineral or organic material prized for its beauty, durability, and rarity.

GEODE A rock cavity lined with crystals that grow toward the center.

GIRDLE The widest part around the middle of a cut stone, where the top half (the crown) and the bottom half (the pavilion) meet.

HABIT The shape in which a crystal naturally occurs.

IDIOCHROMATIC Describes minerals whose color is part of their chemical composition.

Idiochromatic sulfur

INCLUSIONS Material (usually a mineral) trapped within another mineral.

INTERGROWN When two or more minerals grow together and interlock.

IRIDESCENCE A rainbowlike play of colors on the surface of a mineral.

Iridescent hematite crystals

Calcite crystal

Fluorescent crystal

LAPIDARY A skilled cutter of gemstones to obtain the best optical effect.

LAVA Magma from within Earth that erupts to the surface from volcanoes.

LODESTONE A piece of magnetite, a naturally occurring magnetic iron oxide.

LUSTER The way a mineral shines, affected by how light reflects off the surface of the mineral.

MAGMA Molten rock deep below Earth's surface.

MANTLE The layer of Earth between its core and crust.

MASSIVE A term used to describe minerals that have no particular shape.

MATRIX A term for the main body of a rock.

METAMORPHOSIS Recrystallization in a solid rock, leading to a change in mineral composition and texture, usually caused by high heat.

MICROCRYSTALLINE A mineral structure where crystals are too small to be seen with the naked eye.

MINERAL A naturally occurring inorganic solid with regular characteristics.

MIXED CUT A gemstone cut in which the facets above and below the girdle follow different styles, usually a brilliant cut above and a step cut below.

MOHS' SCALE Devised by Austrian mineralogist Friedrich Mohs to measure mineral hardness according to what they are able to scratch.

NACRE Tiny platelets of calcium carbonate that create the sheen on pearls and some seashells as they reflect light.

OPALESCENCE Milky blue form of iridescence.

OPAQUE Does not let light pass through.

ORGANIC GEM A gem made by, or derived from, one or more living organisms.

PEGMATITE Igneous rocks that may contain very large crystals, formed from the very last water-rich magma to crystallize.

PENDELOQUE CUT Lozenge-shaped cut often used for flawed gems.

PHANTOMS Regular inclusions within a crystal, such as parallel growth layers.

PIEZOELECTRICITY A property of quartz crystals. Pressure on a crystal creates positive and negative charges.

PLEOCHROIC Describes a gemstone that looks as if it is two or more different colors when viewed from different directions.

PRISMATIC Describes a "pencil-like" elongated crystal.

PROPERTY A characteristic of a mineral, crystal, or gemstone, such as its color.

REFRACTIVE INDEX (RI) A measure of how light rays slow down and bend as they enter a gemstone.

RESIN A sticky substance from plants.

RHOMB A shape rather like a lopsided cube.

RIVER GRAVELS Deposits of minerals that have been broken away from their host rock and washed downstream.

ROCK A combination of mineral particles; some contain multiple minerals, some only one. Rocks may be inorganic, chemical, or biological in origin.

ROUGH The natural state of a rock or crystal.

SCHILLER Sheen or iridescence.

SPECIFIC GRAVITY (SG) A mineral property that compares its weight with the weight of an equal volume of water.

SPECTROSCOPE An instrument used to identify different gemstones. It reveals the bands of light that a gem absorbs.

Coral, an organic gem

STEP CUT A rectangular or square-shaped gemstone cut with several facets, parallel to the edges of the stone. It is generally used for colored stones.

STRIATION Parallel lines, grooves, or scratches in a mineral.

SYMMETRY, AXIS OF An imaginary straight line through a crystal. If the crystal were rotated about this line, the same pattern of faces would occur a number of times in a full turn.

SYNTHETIC GEMSTONE An artificial stone that has a chemical composition and properties similar to the natural gem from which it is copied.

Step-cut ruby

TABLE CUT A type of step cut with a square table facet and girdle and parallel square facets.

TRANSLUCENT Material that allows some light to pass through it.

TRANSPARENT Material that allows light to pass through it; it is see-through.

TWINNED CRYSTALS Two crystals of the same mineral that are joined together at a common plane—the twin plane.

VEIN An infilled joint, fissure, or fault. Veins are often made of minerals.

VITREOUS A term used for the glasslike quality of some gemstones. It is used to describe a gem's luster.

Pendeloque cut gemstone

Selenite

Twinned calcite crystals

Nacre inside shell

Index

Acknowledgments

The publisher would like to thank the following people for their help with making the book:
Peter Tandy at the Natural History Museum for his expert advice and help; Karl Shone for additional photography (pp.28–29, 62–63); De Beers Industrial Diamond Division for the loan of diamond tools (p.29); Gemmological Association of Great Britain for the gem certificate (p.57); Keith Hammond for the loan of the beryl crystal (p.21); Nancy Armstrong for the loan of the prospector's brooch (p.41); Dr. Wendy Kirk for assisting with revisions; BCP, Marianne Petrou, and Owen Peyton Jones for checking the digitized files; Sreshtha Bhattacharya for editorial assistance; Saloni Singh for the jacket; and Jo Penning for proofreading and the index.

The publisher would like to thank the following for their kind permission to reproduce their images:
(Key: a-above; b-below/bottom; c-center; f-far; l-left; r-right; t-top)

Alamy Images: Art Collection 3 19br, David Gee 5 59tc, Derek Anderson 71cla, Derek Anderson 58cra, GRANGER - Historical Picture Archive 35br, North Wind Picture Archives 60-61c, John Cancalosi 20cl, History and Art Collection 27bc, The Picture Art Collection 50br, Corbin17 40cb, horst friedrichs 27clb, WILDLIFE GmbH 21br, Michele and Tom Grimm 50tr, Tom Grundy 6-7t, Shawn Hempel 56cl, Classic Image 62br, V&A Images 37br, KPixMining 27r, Halyna Kubei 47clb, Wavebreak Media ltd 31cra, Art of Nature 17cr, Nikreates 46ca, 99Wallchartc, dpa picture alliance 42tr, Greg Balfour Evans 54-55c, The Picture Art Collection 50bl, World History Archive 53tl, Fredrik Stenstrm 32-33b; **Archives Pierre et Marie Curie:** 31bc;

Art Directors & TRIP: 69cr; Bergakademie Freiberg: 12cl; **Bibliotheca Ambrosiana, Milan:** 13cr; **Bridgeman Art Library, London / New York:** Egyptian National Museum, Cairo, Egypt 65tc, Baron Antoine Jean Gros 34bl; **© The Trustees of the British Museum. All rights reserved:** 44-45cb; **F. Brisse, "La Symetrie Bidimensionnelle et le Canada", Smithsonian Institution, Washington DC:** 37tr, 39tl, 42br, 69tr; **Canadian Mineralogist,** 19, 217-224 (1981): 13tc; **© Christie's Images Ltd:** 64tl, 65cb; **Christie's, New York:** 57cl; **© Christie's Images Ltd:** 49bl; Corbis: 64b, 69br; **Crown copyright:** 58cr; **De Beers:** 29cc, 34cr; **DK Picture Library:** Natural History Museum 66c; **Dorling Kindersley:** Dreamstime.com: Oleksandr Delyk / Aleksanderdn 28c, Dreamstime.com: Flynt 31br, Ruth Jenkinson / Holts Gems 16cra, Ruth Jenkinson / Holts Gems 32tl, Dreamstime.com: Juliengrondin 8bl, Colin Keates / Natural History Museum, London 2c, Geoff Dann / Wallace Collection, London 52br, Tim Parmenter / Natural History Museum, London 14cra, 99Wallchartcra, Tim Parmenter / Natural History Museum, London 51bc, Tim Parmenter / Natural History Museum, London 47br, Colin Keates / Natural History Museum 36c, Colin Keates / Natural History Museum 38cl, Dreamstime. com: James Phelps 32tr, Dreamstime.com: Aht Yomyai / Wandee007 28l; **Dreamstime.com:** Patrizio Martorana 18cr, Aleksei Suvorov 24-25b; **Getty Images:** Jean-Pierre Clatot / AFP 48-49c, Luis Acosta / AFP 38crb, Dirck Halstead / Hulton Archive 41cra, Hulton Archive 14tr, Bloomberg 25cr, Contributor 17br, Noppawat Tom Charoensinphon / Moment Open 52cb, Willi Rolfes 60cl, Chiara Salvadori 22-23c, Kim Steele 20-21c, STR 58cr, Kriangkrai Thitimakorn 25ca, UniversalImagesGroup 31bc; **Getty Images / iStock:** Mongkolchon Akesin 36-37c, BiancaGrueneberg 63cr,

Feblacal 63tl, 99Wallchartbl, inusuke 55tc, Ozzuboy 59br, V&G Studio 47cb, Huw Thomas 54bc, 99Wallchartcrb; **Mary Evans Picture Library:** 38/39crb, 57tr, 58c, 61tr, 61clb; **Fondation M.S.A.:** lltl; **Michael Freeman:** 25tc, 37c; **Robert Harding Picture Library:** 44tr, 51tl; **Ernst A. Heiniger:** 39br; **Image Bank/Lynn M. Stone:** 33cr; **India Office:** 56tr; **Kobal Collection:** 35ct; **Kodak Ltd:** 63c; **Kunsthistoriches Museum, Vienna.** Photo: Courthault Institute of Art: 40clb; **Lauros-Giraudon:** 34bl; **S. E. Little: Octopus card Ltd** 28clb; **Mansell Collection:** 45c, **Moebius/ Exhibition Bijoux Cailloux Fous, Strasbourg:** 10bc; **Mario Berta Battiloro:** Marino Menegazzo 52tr; **Museum national, d'Histoire Naturelle, Paris:** 48cr; **National Gallery:** 50bl; **Natural History Museum:** 15tr, 19tr, 19c, 40bl, 51br, 68tl / **Frank Greenaway FRPS:** 11bl, 21bc,/ P.Krishna, SS Jiang and A.R. Land: 21tc; **Phototake, NYC/ Yoav Levy:** 30cr; **Réunion Des Musées Nationaux Agence Photographique: Musée de Louvre** 69bc, 69clb; **Royal Geographical Society:** 39tc; **The Metropolitan Museum of Art:** Purchase, Lila Acheson Wallace Gift, Acquisitions Fund and Mary Trumbull Adams Fund, 2015 38cr; **Tokyo Tech Museum:** Tokyo Institute of Technology 30br; **Science Photo Library:** 9tr, 14bl, / Dr Jeremy Burgess: 62tr, 63tr, / John Howard: 43cr, PATRICK LANDMANN 34cra, JAVIER TRUEBA 9l; **Stan Celestian:** Flickr 17cla, 70bc; **Sigalit Landau in the Dead Sea:** Shaxaf Haber 11tr; **SuperStock:** Jean-Paul Ferrero / Mary Evans Picture Library 40-41tl **Universit Paris Cit:** BIU Sant 36bc; **Victoria and Albert Museum:** 51cr; Zefa/ Leidmann:32tl, /Luneski:60cl.

Illustrations: Thomas Keenes.

All other images © Dorling Kindersley